a little eXtra

Linda Mae

Copyright Linda Mae 2001 ©
linda@soloplus.fsnet.co.uk
www.geocities.com/soloplusuk

Produced by Blaisdon Publishing
3 Park Chase, Hornby, Bedale
North Yorkshire DL8 1PR
bruce@blaisdon.force9.co.uk

Reprinted 2006

This Autobiography relates to actual events and nothing is intended to vitiate, or misrepresent any real persons, alive or dead.

ISBN 978 190283813 7
(1 90283813 0)

Front cover picture by Linda Mae
Photograph by Martin Hughes

This book is dedicated to my three children

Lindy Ruth

Philip Andrew

Anna Sarah Elizabeth

and to

My husband, Andrew

Acknowledgements

I would like to thank Timothy Davies for typing the manuscript (with help from Anna), my good friend and neighbour David Bell for proof reading each chapter, and my many friends who have encouraged me to keep writing and complete the book.

Most of all, my thanks go to my husband, Andrew, for all his support.

Christian Artists Seminar, Doorn, August 2000
Tourston Harder as Jesus on the cross

Photo: Edwin Roos

Introduction

'a little eXtra' has been in my mind to write for over ten years now. The original manuscript had three chapters already written but these were torn up and thrown away in 1999 when I came to the conclusion that I would never get round to finishing the book. In 2000, however, I attended the Christian Artists Seminar in Doorn, Holland. Here everyone was given a copy of the book 'Stolen Innocence' written by Ria La Riviere. On reading this, I felt inspired to write my book. In one of the meetings at Christian Artists, we were told that great 'artists' always steal! From Ria, I stole her degree of honesty, and the length of the chapters.

My story as you will see reflects in many of the sketches. Life has been a rich tapestry from which to draw and has helped with the creation of many of the characters. I had originally intended to write my autobiography and then to write a book of sketches, but it has been good to marry the two, along with a few songs and poems.

'A Woman's Touch' is available for booking as a live show by churches, schools, festivals, seminars and conferences worldwide. In addition to the sketches in this book, it contains other sketches and has been performed in the U.K, Holland, Estonia, Cyprus, Romania, Albania and Israel. For bookings, please contact Solo Plus Theatre Company, 222 Cooks Lane, Kingshurst, Birmingham, B37 6NH.

Why 'a little eXtra'? When I first started acting and went to a casting director for parts as a walk-on artist, otherwise known as a 'supporting artist', or 'extra' she took one look at me and said 'You're very little, I don't know what we can cast you as'. Then she added, 'Well I suppose everyone is more or less the same height sat down – I'm sure we'll find you something! True to her word, she did find me plenty of work. Another reason? The Holy Spirit is more than 'a little extra' in my life for which I am very thankful. God has given me so much. This book is my way of giving something back.

Contents

Chapter

	Acknowledgements	5
	Introduction	7
	Illustrations	11
	Foreword	13
1	Grandma	15
2	Drama	19
3	Children	30
4	Mothers	39
5	Fathers	53
6	Boarding School	64
7	Words	76
8	Colour and All That Jazz	86
9	Romania	100
10	Healing	109
11	More Healing	116
12	Yet More Healing	131
13	Mother-in-Law	140
14	Barriers	154
15	Jews	159
16	German	179

Illustrations

Christian Artists Seminar, Doorn, August 2000 6

Matthew and Cameron 18

Herod's Wife from "A Woman's Touch" 23

My children – Anna (5), Philip (6) and Lindy (8) 33

My Mother and I 45

Cousin Susan, sister Letitia and myself 45

My Family 46

My family the one time I met them all 46

My father, Max Garbe 58

My father and I at Lyme Regis in Dorset 59

Me at Boarding School (Ballerina) 67

Me at Boarding School (Celery) 68

My wedding to Andrew on August 19th 1972 89

As the Samaritan Woman at the Well 99

As Mary at the Cross 108

As Sarah in 'Mud and Stars' 134

As Esther in a scene from 'Hadassah' 168

Nick Breakspear Jones as Habal 169

Foreword

a little eXtra

This is an unusual book, full of heart and warmth, but very difficult to classify. Its kaleidoscopic array of approaches and styles of writing suggests to me a hall of mirrors, each one reflecting a facet of the author and her world. As she herself says, and I readily identify with this from my own writing, it is neither easy nor necessary to tease out fact from fiction in the songs and sketches and poems that fill these pages. Certainly, there is a story of physical and mental pain and searching and emotional compromise, but there is also the revelation of a spirit that knows light and life and the laughter of God in the midst of a very tough journey. All the best Christians have had spiritual heart surgery. It takes away their illusions, but it does make them dependent on and thankful to the great surgeon. Here is one of the survivors, tears in her eyes and a smile on her face, with something to say to us. I commend this book to you.

Adrian Plass

Chapter 1

Grandma

What a blessing grandparents can be. My early memory of one grandma, my mother's mother is making mud pies on her hearth when I was three or four years old. That is all I remember. Rumour has it that whenever I went walkabout, which was often, I could usually be found in the little church over the road, in the days of course when all churches were open. I had found sanctuary. God's hand on me at an early age? After all none of my family went to church. Much later at about fourteen years old I received a present, the only one I ever received from her. Since leaving and going to live with my father and stepmother, I only saw her a handful of times and that was as an adult. The present was a scripture birthday book. The verse for January 22nd, my birthday, was 'Love your enemies, bless them that curse you, do good to them that hate you, and pray for them which despitefully use you, and persecute you.' Matt *5* verse 44. How apt.

My other grandma, my stepmother's mother, was always knitting me jumpers and cardigans when I was little. If ever I went shopping with her, she would stop at the cake shop and let me choose the cake I wanted and eat it straight away. A small thing but never to be forgotten.

When I was older – a student – I stayed with her for a night. On going to bed, I shouted 'See you in the morning', to which she replied in amusement, 'Well I certainly hope so!' When I got up in the morning ready to travel back to Teacher's

Training College in York, she presented me with about a dozen small cakes that she had baked. 'These can't be for me', I said instinctively. 'Well they are certainly not for anyone else!' she exclaimed. I was not used to such kindness. It makes me cry even now just to think about it. On my fifteenth birthday, I came downstairs in the morning to find that the rest of the family had gone out. There were no cards and no presents left for me to open, and none materialised later. That is why such simple things as birthday cakes and presents, years later meant, and mean, so much to me.

My other grandma in East Germany, my father's mother, who I only saw once, was just pleased to see me, and concerned. We couldn't speak because of the language barrier, but I knew.

Now I am a grandma with two beautiful little grandsons aged three and four I try to do little things for them to let know how special, how precious and treasured they both are.

My favourite occupation, among many, is to sing to them – 'Granny, granny loves Matthew/Cameron, yes she does, yes she does. Granny, granny loves Matthew/Cameron, yes, she does, and yes, she does. Granny, granny loves Matthew/Cameron, yes, she does, and yes, she does. And granny wants Matthew/ Cameron to love her too.'

Followed by 'grandad loves, mummy loves, daddy loves etc. and Jesus loves'– not necessarily in that order! Matthew from a very early age used to sing the 'too' at the end of each verse. The first time Cameron heard the song at two years old he said 'that's a nice song granny!', and the look of well being on his face as he listened was a picture.

My aim is to build them up so they won't suffer the feelings of inferiority I suffered for a lifetime and even now have to fight against. I often say to them 'Do you know you are wonderful, gorgeous, brilliant, fantastic.... etc', using whatever words come to mind at the time. Or I say, 'Are you wonderful?' to which they answer, 'yes', then I add more and more edifying words for them to affirm, adding, ' Do you know I'm a very lucky grandma to have two such beautiful grandsons?' – and I am!

A bit extreme you may think? Better that than negative words that destroy and hinder lives. At the age of five, I asked my grandma, my stepmother's mother, why my mother had kept my sister and not me. I have never forgotten her reply, which was well intentioned, but misguided – your little sister was pretty with curly hair, and she didn't have a bad leg'. No hurt was intended, she was no doubt trying to brush away the problem as lightly as possible, and make it seem trivial and unimportant; for the reality was my mother had had to get married, and I believe had never been able to forgive me for this. In a letter from my mother in 1996, she said, 'When I gave you away to Mary, I gave you away. I never want to see or hear from you ever again.'

Grandma never knew the result of the words she spoke that day. From that moment on, I hated myself for not having curly hair, for being ugly (as I now assumed I must be, for if not, surely my mother would have kept me, too?), and most of all for having cerebral palsy that meant I had to wear a calliper. I couldn't expect my poor mother to want a reject like me. She deserved better. She was not to blame. It was my fault. That was my reasoning from that day on, until years later when I discovered the truth. If only that innocent half-truth had never been told!

Matthew and Cameron

Chapter 2

Drama

From the age of, seven I knew that I wanted to be an actress. Deep inside I knew that it is what I should be – what I really wanted. But what do you do when your self-confidence is non-existent. When by the age of nine you have short-cropped hair, glasses, and a calliper. Hardly actress material when the world focuses on glamour!

So, I became a teacher because I wanted to help, to communicate, but God brought it full circle. I went from someone wanting to act to being a teacher, who then became an actress working with a Theatre in Education Company in Special schools, which is how I got my Equity card, to someone who then became a supply teacher in Special schools while following an acting career. Quite a perfect situation I would say, but then God our Father is like that.

I believe He always wants us to become what we really are; to become 'us'. The people He made us to be – not what others expect us to be, or want us to be. We need to fulfil our destiny. I used to say I was a teacher who acts. Now I say I'm an actress who teaches which is the way I believe it should be – acting being the priority.

As a student, I used to go to the theatre often hoping this would satisfy my creativity. Later I also joined an amateur drama group hoping that my thirst for acting would be quenched. But it was agony being an audience member when you are dying to act, and I found that the more performing I did the more I wanted to do, and to a higher standard. I felt I just couldn't win!

One day in desperation I prayed, 'Lord please either take away this desire to act because it's killing me, or show me in a way that I can't possibly mistake that you want me to be an actress.' I then forgot about my prayer being a mother with three young children at that time.

Less than a month later, we were at a large Christian Crusade called the 'Good News Crusade' run by Don Double. At the first meeting, someone announced that there was to be some drama workshops. I found myself arguing with God. 'I've already decided what meetings I want to go to' (which was a first for me. I was never usually that organised!) 'Anyway, there will be loads of women all wanting to take part. It's a waste of time me going!' But as you might guess, I ended up there. To cut a long story short I was given the lead role in an improvised performance in front of several thousand people.

I was the 'mother' and everything depended on me. I was responsible for starting the piece off, keeping it going and concluding it. Here I must add that I hate improvisation. I have been known to turn back from auditions not being able to face the improvisations involved.

I was so nervous at the thought of performing that at one time I asked my husband to take us home. I'm so pleased he didn't. As the actors walked up the steps on to the stage one of them placed his hand on my shoulder and prayed for me.

Once on the stage, the improvisation just seemed to 'happen'. I found myself delivering sentences and saying, 'That was good, Lord, I would never have thought of that!' It was a very strange experience. I felt almost as if I was out of my body, a spectator, while at the same time, performing.

When we had finished, Don Double asked people who had felt God ministering to them through the performance to stand up. Many did. He also told them that it was the best piece of drama he had ever seen.

While on stage, I felt an incredible sense of well-being and found myself thinking, 'This is where I belong'. I love my cups of tea, but in those days, if I was in a café and thought someone was watching, I would do without another cup of tea rather than walk across to the counter to be served, as I was so painfully aware of my cerebral palsy – my clumsiness. Looking back, I am amazed that I actually performed in front of so many people.

Returning home, I started private drama lessons. Then one day as I was watching an episode of 'This Is Your Life' about the actor Donald Sinden. I found myself thinking, 'I've got to go to drama school!' I applied to a few and was accepted by the 'Birmingham Theatre School' for a two-year full time acting course. My husband was horrified. We lived in York, three hours away. It would mean selling our home and he would need to get a new job. At the time I was not working. And we had three children of twelve, ten and eight.

We moved to Birmingham finding a house to buy in one day. It had not even been put up for sale when we bought it. Our house in York sold quickly. I moved with the children, and after two weeks of commuting to York, my husband got a job at the Botanical Gardens in Birmingham – the best job he had ever had! If he had said that I could not go to drama school, I don't know what would have happened. Thankfully, we never had to find out. I know I would have gone anyway no matter what. At this point in my life, I had to be true to myself; otherwise, I felt that I would die. All my life I had tried to be someone I was not, tried to live up to other peoples expectations – and the time had come for this to stop. Creativity will out. I had tried to deny it, ignore it, suppress it, but thank God, I had failed!

Herod's Wife from "A Woman's Touch"
(Picture by Yorkshire Evening Press, York ©)

Sketch:

Mary Magdalene

Enter Mary wearing a short black and gold dress, fishnet stockings and gold high-heeled shoes. She has a strawberry mark down one side of her face and neck and walks with a limp.

Mary, Mary Magdalene – that's my name. I expect some of you 'ere know me – if you know what I mean. Don't expect you to admit it though, not with your wives and girlfriends around. Don't you worry, sir, your secret is safe with me. Expect your wondering what I'm doing 'ere. Well, I've been invited. This is the place where people come to talk about Jesus – Jesus of Nazareth isn't it? Well I knew Him. Not in the Biblical sense of course. No. Not like with all my other men.... But I knew Him all right! I suppose you could call me one of His disciples. I've been called worse I can tell you, far worse! Or one of His apostles. His first apostle. Yeah, that'd be about right. That would be about correct. His first apostle! You don't believe me, do you? Oy, what do you think you're looking at. I didn't come 'ere to be stared at. I'm not something the cat's dragged in you know! I've got feelings just like everyone else. Don't let this deceive you *(she points at her birthmark).* You think your better than me, don't you? More respectable. Well, let me tell you.... What's the point? You're all the same: Just 'cos you've got yer posh clothes, yer nice house, and your one point two kids you think your better than me. Well let me tell you something – you're not. It's what's on the inside that counts! Ever 'eard the saying, 'Don't judge a book by it's cover'? Well, I wish more people 'ad. Most of you don't know the first thing about me. Most of you don't know the 'alf of it. Most of you don't know you were born... with 'mummy' and 'daddy' doting over you since the day you arrived. How would you feel if you were born looking like this, eh? (*points to birthmark*). Mum took one look, screamed and dropped me, dropped me like a hot brick, or so I'm told. She didn't want no ugly daughter. She couldn't cope – so I had to suffer. Soon after my sister was born, she upped and left us. Took my sister, left me behind. Dad took me on – at a price. 'Yer little sister was pretty with curly hair and she didn't have no deformed leg that's why she took her'. So that was it, I was the ugly duckling – substandard and deformed. No wonder they all called me names – 'Frankenstein, spastic, shortie, ugly.' The times I wanted to put a paper bag over me 'ead so no one could see me, so no one would know who I was!

I didn't really blame me mum. It's just it hurt so much. I loved 'er yer see. And I couldn't help being ugly. It wasn't my fault. Think mum thought it was hers though – that somehow she was being punished for 'er not being married or something. Oh, they did get married just before I was born, but the guilt was still there. And she didn't want no 'reject' reminding her of it every day of 'er life and so she left, and who can blame her. Didn't do much better with dad. He didn't say much, but I knew I was a big disappointment to him. After all, he wanted a son and ended up with me! It wouldn't 'ave been so bad if I'd been a pretty daughter. He may 'ave learnt to love me then, or at least I could 'ave made him proud of me. But what chance did I stand, I ask you! He was stuck with me and I could tell he resented it. Seemed to think it was a reflection on him. I loved him dearly. But he never knew. I could never tell him. I loved them both but I never let on. I was the black sheep of the family – a disgrace. I wouldn't 'ave wished me on my worst enemy never mind on those I loved. I was so ashamed that I hid away inside myself. They never knew who I really was. And now it's too late; Dad's dead, and Mum still doesn't want to know. I've tried, God knows I've tried – but short of a miracle....

'Love your neighbour as yourself we're told, but how could I? Life was so unfair. I would stand in front of a mirror looking at the thing staring back at me and blame God. Why? Why hadn't he made me pretty like my sister then perhaps mum would have wanted me? What had I done to deserve this – this mark of his disapproval? After all, I hadn't asked to be born. Perhaps I shouldn't 'ave been born. In God's perfect law I would 'ave been conceived in wedlock or not at all, so maybe this was my punishment – my mark of Cain that would dog me for the rest of my life? Every photograph, every relationship was a reminder of what I was – a misfit. How could anyone love me in this world of Cindy dolls and 'perfection'? Everyone needing to be 'model' proportions 34-24-36. Ring a bell lads? How does that make you feel? It sent me in to fits of depression as I remember. Then one day as I was sitting in a bar drowning my sorrows, this fella came up to me. He was a real smooth talker. Told me that it was what was on the inside that counts. That he could tell that I was a warm, caring person. And I fell for it hook, line and sinker. I was only fourteen. I'd borrowed my friend's things while she weren't looking, stole some make up and tarted myself up. I just wanted someone to kiss me, to hug me, to touch me, to care. No one had ever done that from as far back as I can remember. I felt starved of affection, of physical contact and I had to do something or I felt I would die. Once a few weeks earlier, someone had squeezed past me in a crowded room accidentally putting their hand on my shoulder. It was like an electric shock. I didn't know what had hit me. I rushed into the ladies and bawled like a three-year-old. I reckon I was in shock. No one had ever touched me before. Well, I couldn't believe my luck when this good-looking chap came up and said all this stuff to me. Whether it was the drink I don't know, but I believed every word of it. Thought I'd fallen in love and that he had to; that is until a few weeks later when I heard him laughing and joking with his mates, calling me a fat little freak! I couldn't understand it. I'd given him everything and this is how he repaid me – by laughing at me, mocking me. I think they all mocked me and made fun of me just like when I was at school. But I was too stupid to realise it, or too trusting. I wasn't going to have anything more to do with men after that I can tell you, but – but the loneliness got the better of me. And I kept telling myself that the next one would be different. I kept hoping for better. Surely somebody, somewhere would love me sooner or later? So one affair led to another and then another. Then I met Joe, he introduced me to the 'game'. Even there, I was a laughing stock. "We don't want no midgets round 'ere," he said when he first saw me. "You wouldn't be so bad if you had some length to yer leg, girl. 'Ere, wear these shoes, and hide that face, there's a good girl." You should have seen them shoes. No one could walk in heels so high. I wear these... it's the best I can do.

Well that would have been my life mapped out if it hadn't been for one thing. I met Jesus. I literally bumped into Him one day as I was rushing out for a fix. I was into drugs by this time, and I was practically anorexic. No one was going to call me a fat freak ever again. Well Jesus, He stooped down and helped me pick up the fistful of money I'd dropped, and looked right into my eyes, right in to my soul. It was as if He knew everything about me – everything I'd ever thought or done. He knew, and yet I knew He didn't condemn me. That He loved me. I'd never experienced anything like it. My heart almost stopped beating, time stood still for what seemed like an eternity. He must have seen the state I was in, but there was no condemnation in His look, only pity and compassion. It was as if He understood and 'forgave' me. Well as you can imagine, I didn't get my fix – I didn't need it. I just left everything there and then and followed Him. His disciples Peter, James and Judas and some of the others weren't too pleased, but they couldn't do anything about it because they could see that their Master had accepted me just as I was, and they knew that they should do the same. I've never been able to understand it really. Jesus was so holy and good and yet He accepted me. Then I heard Him say, 'Those who are well do not need a physician only those who are sick', 'I have not come to call the righteous but sinners to repentance.' Well I understood that all right, He was talking about me and all those like me. Well, I followed Him for over two years and learnt all sorts of things. I learnt that God looks on the heart and not the outward appearance for a start, and I suppose I learnt to 'love myself'. Jesus helped of course. Like the time I went with the other women to put spices on His Body after He had been crucified and laid in the grave. As you know, the gravestone had been rolled away – God knows how and when we went inside the tomb the Body wasn't there. The grave-clothes were there all neat and tidy, but there was no Body. The others were so upset that they went back home, but I stayed behind in the garden. I had to know where the Body of my Master was. I know it sounds silly but I felt that He had died just because of me, just because of my sin. Then I saw the gardener, or so I thought, and asked Him where He'd put the Body. He said my name 'Mary' and I knew at once that it was Jesus. I ran to Him to touch Him, to hug Him. But He said 'Do not touch Me, for I have not yet ascended to Him who is your Father and My Father, your God and My God. But go to My disciples and tell them that I am alive – that I have risen from the dead just as I said I would.' *(defiantly to audience)* So you see, I was His first apostle. He could have chosen any one to tell His disciples that He was alive – but He chose to choose me.

Chapter 3

Children

When we were married, one of the choices of Psalms was Ps. 127 verses 3-5.

'Lo, children are a heritage of the Lord: and the fruit of the womb is his reward. As arrows are in the hand of the mighty man; so are children of the youth. Happy is the man that hath his quiver full of them.'

I didn't want a quiver full of them! In fact, I was not sure I wanted any. I certainly did not want an unwanted child for the child's sake. I knew only too well what that felt like. But surely if you were married you were meant to have children? The only thing I could think to do was pray. It went something like this – 'Lord, I suppose I should have children, but You know that I don't want an unwanted child so please give me the desire for a child before I have one.' Over a year later, when praying with my husband and a couple of close friends, to my amazement I found myself praying for a child. I hadn't intended to – the desire for a child suddenly overwhelmed me. Little did I know at the time, but I was already expecting Lindy Ruth, our firstborn. When I went for the test my husband did not have to ask for the result, my face said it all, I was so delighted.

Philip Andrew was born next, just under two years later. Every time I saw a baby on television, I would burst into tears. That was my clue that I probably wanted to have another child! We tried for three or four months and there was still no baby. To me it seemed like the end of the world. I asked our church prayer group to pray for us and I put my order in. I wanted a boy with 'red' curly hair. My husband had ginger hair and I loved it. I had in fact had three boyfriends with ginger hair, all Christians and all with birthdays in May! I married the third one, by which time I had admitted to myself, and others, that I like people with ginger hair. I had not realised it before.

After asking for prayer, I began to realise that maybe I should not just pray for a baby and expect it to happen. Maybe God only wanted me to have the one. When I really accepted this as a possibility giving over my will to God, the next thing I knew was that I was pregnant with Philip. People told me that he could not possibly be born with 'red' hair because that always skips a generation, and in any case 'he' might be a 'she', to which I thought, 'You don't know my God!' Sure enough Philip was born with 'red', slightly curly hair for which he has never forgiven me, even in his late teens trying to do an 'Anne of Green Gables' by dying it brown! But I love it, and I love him.

Number three was a complete shock. It was in my days of being naively 'Christian'. If God created the world, I reasoned, then all I have to do is pray and I won't have any more children! I was finding two quite a handful at the time, with Philip waking up every two hours, and not being able to get a good night's sleep. Then just when he was coming up to one year old and things were getting a little easier, I discovered that I was expecting Anna.

My doctor, a Christian from our church, immediately offered me an abortion. I didn't even answer him. I was so disgusted. It was not something I would consider for a second. He apologised hastily explaining that it as his duty as a doctor to give me the option. I was not strong enough physically, mentally or emotionally to have children, and certainly no more than one. It was no disgrace – some people were just like that. Why then had it taken him until now to tell me? But I'm glad it had because now I was having three whatever happens.

I like to imagine God thinking – 'Linda thinks she only wants two children, but I know that she will really love to have an Anna.' How true. After the initial shock, I couldn't wait for Anna Sarah Elizabeth to be born. Why does it have to take nine months anyway!

Needless to say, I am so proud of all my children. Lindy is married, a wonderful mother of two beautiful boys, has a degree, and is a teacher. More importantly, she is very kind and caring and has been since childhood. Philip is engaged to Jenny who is an excellent cellist; he is following a career in computers and has a terrific sense of humour. Anna is an accomplished musician studying music composition at Coventry University. As a child she brought me so much joy – she was my little ray of sunshine who brightened up each day. How dare a doctor suggest that we should be denied this treasure, or any of our treasures? All children I believe are gifts from the Lord no matter what the circumstance of their birth. My mother chose to give me the gift of life and I am thankful; for things could have been so different for both myself and Anna. Ultimately though, it was God who purposes that we should be born – 'All our days were written in His Book, when as yet there was none of them,' Psalm 139 verse 16.

I was less than two pounds in weight when I was born and humanly speaking, should not have survived. But God, I believe, had other plans!

From left to right:

My children – Anna (5), Philip (6) and Lindy (8)

Philip looking very proud of his sisters; like the cat that's just swallowed the canary!

Poem:

Mother

Written by Linda Mae after the birth of her daughter
Lindy Ruth on 1.12.74

To be a mother is a gift from God,
Perishable. Cherishable
The choice is yours.
God bestows the gift –
BUT how is it accepted?
Joy, wonderful joy
Over the birth of a child
Over the wonder of motherhood
So often taken for granted?
Ponder a while on this gift –
What is the gift you have been given?

A child
New born
Tender
Impressionable.
To bring up in the knowledge
And love of God
To care for
Love
Cherish
Direct
And guide
In the ways
And paths of God

What a gift – what a God!

Sketch:

Elizabeth

I was the first one she told. Apart from Joseph that is. After all, I am her cousin. She came to stay with me you know. Me – the one known as 'the barren one'. The failure. Unable even to conceive, unable to bear a child, to bear a son. No one actually ever said that of course but I felt it in my spirit, and I could see it in their eyes. Even in Zachariah, my husband, a godly man. Oh, he tried to hide it of course, but I could see the pain, the disappointment in his eyes as month after month, year after year went by. It was so hard for me, so very hard for me and it didn't get any easier with age – harder in fact, as time runs out, hope diminishes. At times, I felt my heart would break in two! Watching others nursing their children, seeing young children laughing and playing in the street, catching a father's proud look as his son entered the Temple for the first time, a mother's proud glance at a daughter about to be wed. Constant, constant reminders.

Oh, it can't have been easy for Zachariah either the jibes about not being able to father a child, the shame. We were the talk of our neighbourhood for years. You can imagine the looks I got, the nods, the whispers. I don't know which was worse that or the Job's comforters, the ones who pretended to understand... How could they – with their children in tow!

You must have heard of me – Mary's cousin Elizabeth the one who was barren, but who then by the grace of God became pregnant. And at my age. Who would have thought it? It was a miracle! When Zachariah first told me that I was to have a son! That an angel had appeared to him while he was in the Temple telling him that his prayer had been answered! I could hardly believe it! I didn't say that, though. I didn't dare! I just thought, "What? At my age you must be joking! It's impossible. Both of us were well past the age..." But then Zachariah had been struck dumb for not believing the angels words and I didn't want the same to happen to me. He had to write the message down for me. Could it be possible that I really was to have a child, a son after all these years?

When Mary came to visit it was such a comfort to me. I knew by then that it really was true. That at long last I was pregnant. I think Mary needed some space poor girl. Needed someone she could talk to. Someone who would believe her; who would understand her. An angel appeared to her too, you see, came and spoke to her just as one had spoken to Zachariah. Not long after Joseph had left, she said. She was alone in the house praying. It was barely light. She was always praying, our Mary. We used to joke and say she prayed too much. That her thoughts were always in another world. She was a dreamer all right, but then so was our ancestor, Joseph, and look what happened to him! If Mary had her way, I'm sure she would have become a Levite, spending all her time in the Temple day and night praising and worshipping Jehovah, studying the Law and the Prophets. She would have loved that. I always said she should have been a boy! But then none of this could have happened.

She said that the angel Gabriel had told her not to be afraid for she would bear God's Son. The Holy Spirit would overshadow her, he said, and she would become pregnant. She told him that she was willing to do God's will, whatever the cost... but that she could not understand how this could possibly happen? I know just how she feels! Then he told her about me being six months pregnant, saying that with God nothing is impossible. 'Let it be done unto me according to God's will,' Mary replied, and now she is pregnant. And yet, she has known no man. Another miracle? 'A virgin shall conceive and bear a Son,' our scriptures say. I wonder... could Mary be...?

The angel Gabriel... that was the same angel who appeared to Zachariah... who told him to name our son John.

When Mary walked through the door my baby, John, leapt for joy in my womb. The angel Gabriel told my husband so much about our son. He would be our joy and our delight, many would rejoice because of his birth, he would be great in the sight of the Lord and filled with the Holy Spirit from birth. He would bring many in Israel back to their God, and he would prepare the way of the Lord...the Messiah. And Mary's child, what of Him? 'You will call His name Jesus,' the angel said, 'for He shall save His people from their sins'.

Poem:

Marriage

Written by Linda Mae for her daughter Lindy Ruth's wedding 20.1.96

Two hearts entwined as one

Two minds seeking the truth in love

Two souls reaching out to God in their commitment.

Their hearts,

minds,

bodies,

souls

Become one

In this great sacrament

MARRIAGE.

Chapter 4

Mothers

It was Mothering Sunday again and I was sat in church trying not to 'feel'. Every year it brought it back – 'I want my mother'. By now, I was married and had my own children but it made no difference! I wanted my mother. Although she had left me when I was three years old and did not ever try to get in touch I still wanted to find her. I had tried once or twice over the years, contacting the Salvation Army, trying to find out the address from my grandma, and at one time even thinking of contacting my dad for any information he could give. Every time it failed. The Salvation Army could give me no information, my grandmother had moved and when I tried later she had died, and my dad died of a heart attack while I was still trying to trace where he lived. As you can imagine these deaths happening each time I tried to trace her put me off for many years. That coupled with the fact that I had contacted her twice in my life already and the results had not been at all encouraging. At the age of five, I had sent her a present for my sister – it was a lovely gift that someone had sent me for my birthday, but I wanted to make contact so much that the nuns at the boarding school helped me to send it. I waited and waited for a letter of thanks but it never came. Then at about nine years old, I found her address. She had written to my dad to ask for money to help with bringing up my sister. It was a strange episode. As I came down to breakfast, my stepmother quickly slipped a letter into her dressing gown pocket. I knew instinctively that it was from my mother. As far as I know she had never written before and has never written since so why it should even pass my mind I don't know. When they went out later I searched for and found the letter. I wrote to my mother. The reply came back – 'Don't call me Mum, call me Aunty Dot.' I never wrote again.

Maybe her new husband didn't know I existed. My half brothers only found out when they were in their late teens. My sister was too young when mum left to remember me. They were given various tales as to who the little girl in the photos was.

When my dad died I was not invited to the funeral. The reason was simple. On telephoning his third wife (my half brother on my stepmother's side had been told of his death) to see if I could have a small memento of my father as I had almost nothing belonging to him, I was told he only had one daughter, Sarah, my half sister! She obviously didn't know about me at all.

One time at a small prayer group, I shared that I was hoping to trace my mum. The leader, a lady who at the time knew nothing about me, apologised saying I don't know why but I believe this scripture is for you – 'Hearken, O daughter, and consider, and incline thine ear; forget also thine own people, and thy father's house; So shall the King greatly desire thy beauty: for He is thy Lord; and worship thou Him.' Psalm 45 verses 10 & 11. The same verse that I had read a year or two earlier when considering finding my mother! It had been so powerful on that occasion that I had proceeded no further.

Now however sat in church on that Mothering Sunday it felt that the time was right. This time it was so easy. I looked in the telephone book under my grandmother's surname 'Partlow', and spoke to the first name I found, briefly explaining the situation. 'I'm your Uncle Stan,' the voice announced. Now it was my turn. 'But I only have one Uncle and he died in a swimming accident when he was with my dad at the swimming baths.' My grandmother had shown me a photo and told me the story one of the few times I had seen her.

Another secret that had been kept from us by my father who it seems never wanted anyone to find out the truth about anything. It appears that my Uncle had been living only a few miles from where I had been brought up. No wonder it had been kept secret.

My Uncle got in touch with my mother on my behalf checking for me beforehand that she really did want to see me, and a meeting was arranged. My husband and I travelled to Whitchurch where she now lived. Everyone was there – my mother, her husband Cliff, my sister Letitia with her husband, Elwyn, and Gary and Peter my half brothers. We were made welcome. The photos came out and I asked a few questions. I had brought my camera with me and was anxious to take a few photos of my family. 'Don't worry', my mother said, 'if they don't turn out there will be other opportunities'. 'No there won't,' I thought to my amazement, and it was true. The family would not be together again.

I saw my mother two or three times more. Once, when it was her birthday. I had discovered that she liked *Babycham* so I arrived with a bottle, plus a birthday cake, card, and a present – a beautiful china mug with 'mother' and a verse written on it. It was my way of saying, 'I forgive you for the past. Let's start afresh. I accept you as my mother.'

Shortly after this, I received a terrible letter saying that if I needed a mother then there was something wrong with me. She never wanted to see me again and I was not allowed to write or contact her in any way. None of her family, not even her husband, knew anything about the letter and they were all shocked when I told them. Effectively, she had cut me off from all of my newfound family. Thank God that He had prepared me. I was still devastated though. What kept me going at the time was being involved in the Coventry Mystery Plays. It stopped me brooding.

My children were all very upset. One minute they had three new aunts and uncles, plus eight new cousins, and a grandmother and grandfather, and the next minute there was no one. Everyone had been great, everyone that is, except my mother. I tried to give her a hug as I left on the first occasion. I did, but it felt as if she was a million miles away. There was no warmth whatsoever.

At first, I could not understand why I was allowed to see her only to be rejected again. It did not seem to make any sense. Now I can see several good things that have come out of it. I had discovered my roots – I had met my biological mother and this in itself was important. My curiosity had been satisfied. I now understood who I was a little more and I needed that. When I first met my mother, I could not believe it. We were so totally different, worlds apart. I remember watching her and thinking, 'You're my mother?!' I knew that if we were left together in a room, we could not have managed to talk for even half an hour – and I can talk to anyone!

She was virtually a recluse. She went out once a fortnight to the hairdressers and that was it. She seemed to love animals and have no time for people, not even her grandchildren. Cliff, her husband, was the opposite – a lovely man who genuinely welcomed us into the family. It was strange – my half brother Gary I felt I had known all my life. We could have talked forever. My half brother Peter was very shy, but I liked him very much. My sister Letitia was nice, but again we had nothing whatsoever in common. Gary, when he knew he was going to meet us, excitedly told all his friends that he was going to meet his sister! I remember saying to him the first time we met that my sister was the lucky one going with mum and that I had drawn the short straw. I will never forget his reply – 'If you hadn't gone away you would not be the person you are today, and I like that person.' It reminded me of the story of Joseph who had been sold into slavery by his brothers and later realised that it was God and not man who had placed him where he was.

If I had not gone, I would not have attended boarding school and maybe never become a Christian. It doesn't bear thinking about! In fact, most of the things I had done in my life would probably never have happened – being a teacher, becoming an actor, marrying Andrew, having our three children, having my two grandchildren – how dreadful!

Another good thing that happened as a direct result of the rejection was that my stepmother and I seemed to have a different relationship from then on. Thinking back it must have been hard to bring someone up and be their 'mother', all the time knowing that they are wanting to be with their natural mother. It had never occurred to me before. In reality, my stepmother had been and still is my 'mother'. After all, she has looked after me from the age of four.

I think I wouldn't have rated very high in the 'mother' stakes had there been one. I did my best, of course, but was usually either ill or exhausted. Each of my children at one point in their lives have said that I loved the other best, but as they all said it about each other I think they must have been pretty equal! I love Lindy best because she was my firstborn, my answer to prayer. I love Philip best because he is my only son, and an answer to prayer. I love Anna best because she is my bonus, my baby. The eldest is always special. A son is always special. The youngest is always special. A mother should know!

My Mother and I

I was the one on the right, explained away to my half brothers and my sister for years as a 'friend'. In the centre is my younger sister, Letitia, and on the left, wearing glasses, is my cousin, Susan, who died tragically in a car accident as a teenager.

My family the one time I met them all.

Front row left to right:

My sister-in law, Larraine, me, my Mum, my sister, Letitia, and my sister-in-law, Sue, with her youngest child.

Back row left to right:

My brother-in-law, Elwyn, stepfather, Cliff, half-brother, Garry, and half-brother, Peter.

Sketch:

The Letter

(There is a video screen on stage. One side the mum is spotlighted and on the other the daughter crouched on the floor 'reading' the letter)

Mother: Dear Ruth if you are reading this then you have discovered the truth. You have the right to know everything, and as the person who gave birth to you, I have a duty to tell you.

I cannot hope for forgiveness, but I hope that you will one day understand. Your existence was not planned. Far from it. I wish I could say that it was a result of young love, of foolish hearts, but that, too, is not true. I was raped. Brutally raped... by a stranger as I walked home. About seven o'clock one evening. On a country lane. It was the worst moment of my life. His eyes. I will never forget his eyes – cold, staring eyes as long as I live. I cannot forget them. I thought I was going to die!

I was sixteen when I gave birth to you. I was hurt, bitter, filled with hate. I couldn't hold you, touch you, love you. You reminded me of that night, of that man, of my lost innocence. For months, years afterwards I had nightmares – would wake up screaming, shaking – I couldn't face being reminded. I couldn't keep you. The family decided it was best if you were looked after by my brother and his wife.

(VIDEO of baby being handed over to them while song 'Crying Out' is sung by the mother, or alternatively, the music of 'Crying Out' is played)

It was only supposed to be for a while, until I came to terms with what had happened. I was going to take you back, eventually. But every month that passed, it made it easier to forget that you were mine. I used to see you sometimes, playing with the others. And you seemed OK, normal, happy.

Then I got a chance to move away. I met someone who accepted me for who I was, for what I had become. I needed his love. It was the choice I had to make. I know that you will feel let down, rejected – but I gave you the gift of life – I fought to give you that, treasure it! Forgive me, my child, my daughter. And be grateful for the life you now have. I hope that you are happy. All my love, your Mother. (Daughter exits)

(A letter explaining why, with similar words to those written below are what I always hoped I would receive from my mother one day)

Mother: Brave words. Fine sentiments then. But now. What about now? What have I missed? What did I forfeit by giving you away? My child, my daughter growing up. The smiles, the faltering steps, the first words. The hugs, the kisses, little secrets shared, friendship, memories – and for what? Those years can never be regained. They are gone forever, vanished, melted into eternity. I can never reclaim them; I cannot bring them back – ever.

                If only I had been stronger, tried harder, fought longer. Kept the one treasure born out of the evil.

	If only I had believed in mother love, trusted that time would heal, that hurts would disappear, that bonds would be forged with you the innocent, being innocent.
Voice of God:	'I did knit you together in your mother's womb. Your frame was not being hidden from Me when you were being formed in secret and intricately and curiously wrought as if embroidered with various colours. My eyes saw your unformed substance, and in My Book all the days of your life were written before ever they took shape. For I did form your inward parts.'
Mother:	It was your sixteenth birthday yesterday. You were sixteen. Sweet sixteen. The same age as me when I gave bir...I thought it was right at the time. That it was the best thing – the only thing I could do. The guilt I felt at having you. You could not begin to understand. I wanted to rid myself of that guilt. To forget. To persuade myself that it was not my fault. That the rape was not my fault. That I had not asked for it. That I didn't deserve it. That I was not guilty. I know I wasn't, but 'it was your fault; it has to be your fault. You are to blame went round and round in my head taunting me. Crazy I know but these crazy thoughts would not let go. Kept telling me that I got what I deserved. That I should not expect any different, that I was trash, worthless, a loser...and so I gave you away, I lost you.

'Crying Out' sung by the Mother, as a dancer in black dances and the shot of the baby being given away is frozen on screen.

Crying Out

Words by Linda Mae & Anna Appleyard
Music by Anna Appleyard

Verse 1:

I cry out in my heart
With all the pain I find
And pour out my feelings once again.
I give God all my sorrows
I give Him all my fears
And I want to know the reason why I live.

CHORUS:

You are my protection, Lord
You are all I need in my life
Listen to my cry Lord
For I'm helpless, I'm helpless without you.

Verse 2:

Look at me and see the turmoil that I feel
Without You here beside me
I'm alone, I'm afraid.
I'm helpless without You
Imprisoned in my fear
But You could give me hope to carry on.

CHORUS:

Chapter 5

Fathers

It was Father's Day and my Father had died six months earlier. I wandered round the city of York watching people buying cards and presents. It was almost too much. I went into a local church selling tea and coffee and sat down. I looked at the vicar as he walked past. 'Not much point asking for his help,' I thought, 'a typical Anglican vicar!' Suddenly everything got too much and I went and locked myself in the 'Ladies' and wept. Just as I came out who should be passing but the vicar who asked how I was. We went into his study where he talked to me, prayed for me and ministered to me. How wrong I had been!

I went back out to the shops and found myself drawn to a jeweller's shop window. I felt my Father God saying, 'I am your Father. It's Father's Day. I want you to buy a gift for yourself from Me.' I looked and saw a pretty pair of blue earrings and bought them. That was seventeen years ago. I still have one of them decorating a perfume bottle as a reminder of God's love.

My Father died at the age of fifty-five. For a long time I used to look at old people and think, 'It isn't fair. I never had the opportunity to get to know him. Who was he really? What made him behave in the way he did? What did happen in his childhood and teenage years? What was it like being in Germany at that time and being part of the Hitler Youth? What were his dreams and aspirations?' I really did want to know. I had always wanted to know.

I had spent my whole life trying to make him proud of me, and Sarah my half sister had done the same. We had not managed – but then we were girls and so didn't really stand a chance. Only twice did he take notice of me; once when as a teenager, I had my letter printed in the newspaper, and when I told him that I had an interview to go to University. Now I could never make him proud of me – it was too late.

I had always idolised my Father, made excuses for him, reasoned that he must love me really; after all, he had taken me with him, hadn't he? I found out much later that he had got a divorce on the grounds of my mother's cruelty to me through a German court although we were living in England. Did he tell the truth or lies? I will never know.

I don't know how he did it but he always made you feel inferior, not good enough. As a child, I felt sorry for him that he had me as a daughter. After all, he deserved someone pretty and intelligent who he could be proud of, who he could show off to all his friends. By the time I was a teenager, the feeling had got much worse. I remember walking home from school, my footsteps getting slower and slower the nearer I got. 'Any minute now I will be going backwards!' I thought. Then I came up with an idea. I was so ugly that maybe if I put a paper bag over my head with slits for the eyes no one would have to see me. I felt so ashamed of who I was. Then to my dismay I realised that it wouldn't work, as it would only succeed in drawing people's attention to me, and that was the last thing I wanted.

'Praise and worship God your Father,' the leader of the meeting enthused. No chance. That was one thing I had never been able to do! Jesus was great. He was my Friend and my Saviour, and hopefully my Lord. The Holy Spirit was no problem. He was my Guide and my Comforter. But God the Father – that was quite another thing. What would He think of me? I must be doing something wrong. I must be displeasing Him. He certainly couldn't love me. It was too dangerous to risk getting close to Him. I would stick to two out of the three and keep my distance from the Father, after all I had managed it from as far back as I can remember.

All those around me seemed to be praising God the Father. Was I the only one with a problem? I prayed. It had to be dealt with at some time. I didn't want this to last all my life. Then as I looked, I saw an image of my earthly Father (he had already died by this time), as if on a projector screen immediately above my head. He, it seemed, was causing the barrier between myself and Father God. I prayed once more and the image disappeared. From that day on, I was able to praise and appreciate my Heavenly Father without fear.

When my Father died, I was devastated and in mourning for months. I had always loved him very much – too much perhaps. I had put him on a pedestal. With his death however, there came a freedom. A freedom to become whole. It was as if a heavy burden had been lifted. I could breathe at last. The bonds had been cut once and for all.

He had done many things a Father should not have done, and crippled many lives. When I was seventeen and living away from home, I visited my father. He persuaded me to stay overnight and travel home the next day. I agreed, delighted that my father seemed to want to spend time with me. I had naturally expected to stay in the spare room, but to my horror, I found that he had pushed the two single beds in his room together and that he was expecting me to sleep with him! It was very late and there was no one else in the house. I quietly said 'No' and lay awake most of the night praying, and he was powerless to harm me. The next morning he told me never to tell anyone what had happened. However, when he was planning to take my half-brother, Michael, alone on a camping holiday, I felt I had to tell my stepmother, as I was not sure that even Michael would be safe. The reason why I didn't run out of the house or try to phone the police or contact a neighbour when I was with him? I felt that if I'd offered any overt resistance he would have turned violent and even have tried to kill me. After all he had tried to kill my mother, and strangle my stepmother.

For years, I had thought that my half-sister, Sarah Jane, had managed to escape the hurt and abuse being only six years old when he left, but I was wrong. I recently discovered this when reading her account of her life where she tells her side of the story.

'I can't remember much of my childhood, but I do know that my father played a very important part in making it terrible. The funny thing is that I was so browbeaten and insecure that I didn't even know it was terrible until very recently. I have very few memories of my father. A fact until recently I didn't even think about or realize. It was only a recent awakening to a buried memory of him being abusive that made me want to take stock, and I couldn't because I didn't have the information. I wondered why, like Linda, I had always been terrified, or at least nervous of all my friends' and boyfriends' fathers – I just thought it was because I wasn't used to having men around. Well it turns out that we all had to tiptoe around daddy, because if he got irritated or annoyed with us (that included my mum) we would all know about it. So here lies my innate ability, or rather even neediness, to please at all costs to myself and often to friendships and relationships. I have often wondered why men have always ended up (nice men too) wanting to hurt me in some way or another. It was because they could.

My memories of Dad are as follows. I remember him standing in the kitchen with his hands on his hips, looking down at me and saying, 'I just want to get rid of you. I never wanted you in the first place.' I remember myself being playful at the age of about five and hiding under the sofa cushions to pretend to Daddy that I wasn't there. Instead of allowing me to jump up and surprise him, he sat on my head and refused, despite my screams and real distress, to get off. This is a fully-grown man sitting on a five-year-old's head. I was absolutely hysterical with fear and claustrophobia and thought I would die.

I remember my Dad beating up my mum in the garage and throwing her about against the walls and my poor, messed up brother – then only eleven years old – trying to drag him off her. He once took my dog for a walk and then came back without him. He had him put down for no reason at all except that the dog didn't much like him, and one day, he bought me a toy dog to take it's place. He kidnapped me from hospital once. Not because he wanted me, but only to hurt my mother.'

Sarah is only just coming to terms with this now at the age of thirty-seven, after it having taken quite a toll on her life, as it has done on mine. Dad had been in the Hitler Youth and was brought up to believe in the Aryan race. No wonder he hated women so much. My sister and I must have created special problems for him, as I had cerebral palsy and Sarah was asthmatic. According to his family, he remained a Nazi all his life.

One day while I was still at college, my father stood one side of me and my stepmother the other. He was leaving and I had to choose between them. There was no contest. My stepmother needed me and there was no way I could be alone in the same house as him. I have since heard that, as a very young child, he used to beat me and lock me in a broom cupboard in the dark for hours on end. This I do not remember, but I do know that I only ever felt safe if my stepmother was at home and within calling distance. Luckily for me that day – I had no decision to make. He had made it for me.

The saddest thing during these years was that I was powerless to help him, being entangled in the vicious circle myself. I wish I had been stronger for all our sakes.

My father, Max Garbe
second from the right on the back row, under the cross

*My father and I at Lyme Regis in Dorset
smiling for the camera*

Song:

Father

Words by Linda Mae
Music by Anna Appleyard

Chorus: Father – You are my loving Heavenly Father.

You created me, cared for me.

Since the beginning of time.

Verse 1: All the hairs of my head, they are numbered by You

All my days they are written in Your Book

Every step that I take it is ordered by You

Your blessings they never end.

Chorus: repeat

Verse 2: Every word on my tongue, it is known by You

Before it has even yet been spoke

Every thought that I have, it is seen by You

Your love it will never end.

Chorus: repeat

then whisper: ABBA FATHER, FATHER, FATHER, FATHER (declining in volume)

* * * * *

Earthly fathers let us down constantly, but our Heavenly Father is so different. One college holiday I was meant to go home. I really couldn't face it. I was at a youth club where I helped and went into the office and started to read the Bible. As I looked at Isaiah 43, these words became illuminated. It was as if a spotlight had been shined on them. All the rest of the page remained as normal.

'When thou passest through the waters, I will be with thee, and through the rivers, they shall not overflow thee: when thou walkest through the fire, thou shalt not be burned; neither shall the flame kindle upon thee...remember ye not the former things, neither consider the things of old. Behold, I will do a new thing; now it shall spring forth; shall ye not know it? I will even make a way in the wilderness, and rivers in the desert.'

And my Father God was true to His word.

* * * * *

Song:

Do You Doubt Me?

Words by Linda Mae
Music by Linda Mae Anna Appleyard

Verse 1:

    Do you doubt Me, do you doubt My word?
    Do you doubt Me disregarding all you've heard?
    Do you doubt My word?

Verse 2:

    Oh My children how I wish you knew
    Oh My children how I wish you knew
    The love I have for you.

Verse 3:

    Be believers look up and see
    Be believers these things can really be.
    Look up and see.

Chapter 6

Boarding School

I remember being taken into a dark dining room in a strange house one day. This was to be my new home. There was a very large dog Jeff, a Bull Mastiff, who came bounding over to me nearly knocking me flying. He licked my face overjoyed to find a friend. He used to let me ride on his back.

My next memory was being taken into a school hall. Away from Jeff. Away from home. There were girls playing, boarders. I was made to join them. My dad and my stepmother left. I was alone with strangers. There was no one my age. No boarders aged five. And I was a long way from home.

It was a school run by French Roman Catholic Dominican nuns – in Chard, Somerset. They were all very good to me. Sister Gilbert was, I believe, given special care of me. She told me that Jesus loved me. I needed to hear that. 'He died for your sins,' she said, 'He has gone to prepare a place for you in Heaven so that when you die you can go to live with Him forever. If you ask Him to forgive your sins He will, and He will be your Friend for the whole of your life.'

I had never met adults who believed in God before, and thought that if they could serve God and give their lives to Him so wholeheartedly, then so could I. When no one was around, I prayed. I asked Jesus to take away my sins and become my friend for life. And He did. My basic faith has not changed from that day to this and I owe the Roman Catholics a great debt of gratitude.

One of the older girls gave me some pretty rosary beads as a present. They were turquoise. I lost them and so I prayed to St Anthony. I never did find them. I remember saying to God, 'I knew those saints were no good. I'll just pray to my Friend Jesus in future!'

When it was Lent, we had to do good deeds so as to be allowed to take out some of the thorns from Jesus' crown of thorns and so lessen His suffering, and we had to give up things like sweets. There was one nun I was really afraid of. She was the nun that made wonderful bars of homemade toffee, and it was this fact alone that caused me to have any contact with her at all. The poor woman must have wondered what on earth she had done wrong. She was called Sister Lucifer that's all – so I was terrified of her. Fancy being named after Lucifer the devil!

I could not understand some of their teaching. On the one hand, they told me that Jesus loved me and had died for my sins, and on the other they told me that if I did not become a Roman Catholic, being baptised into their faith, I would go to hell. Which one was true? I chose to believe the former.

We were expected to pray to the Virgin Mary in church. There were Roman candles lit in front of her outdoor statue on bonfire night, and there was a small luminous statue/music box that glowed in the dark and could play 'Ave Maria' – eerie, I didn't like any of it. I used to kneel before her statue and say, 'Jesus, you know I am really praying to You, but I don't want to offend these lovely ladies'. We were also expected to kneel and pray in front of statues of some of the saints. I used to close my eyes, pray to Jesus, and hope that when I opened them again, the statues hadn't miraculously come to life, and that they were still only statues. I had been told stories of statues of 'Our Lady' coming to life, as the lady herself appeared and spoke God's messages to people like Joan of Arc and St Bernadette, and as people were healed at Lourdes. I still feel anxiety when going into churches that have icons and statues and pray with my eyes open.

When I went to bed in the dormitory, Sister Gilbert used to tell me that my Guardian Angel would be looking after me while I slept. It made me almost too frightened to close my eyes because when I opened them again I might see the Angel standing at the foot of my bed. I do believe in Guardian Angels, and ministering Angels, and warring Angels but I don't really want to see them. I have friends who have seen Angels and they assure me that it is an awesome and comforting experience. I think I'll just take their word for that! I have a sticker that Lindy brought me back from Germany to put on the rear windscreen of my car. It says in German: *'Fahr' nicht schneller, als Dein Schtzengel fliegen kann'* - 'Don't drive any faster than your Guardian Angel can fly', and I find it a comforting reminder that God is watching over me, as well as a harmless piece of humour.

Boarding school days were happy ones that unfortunately ended after two years when Michael was born. The only minus was the unhealthy sense of guilt their religion instilled, and the negative attitude towards men. They were in the world and you should be polite to them, but it was really best to ignore their existence and have little or nothing to do with them. As I only ever went to all girls' schools, Roman Catholic ones, until I was fourteen, it was quite a shock to go to a Teachers' Training College that was mixed. I have sent all my three children to Roman Catholic schools where they, like me, were extremely happy. The schools teach good moral standards, and treat people with respect acknowledging that we are all different and important to God, and that it is not only academic brilliance that is important. When I say this to my Roman Catholic friends, they are very surprised as their schools were not like that. I guess we were just very lucky.

*Me at Boarding School
as a ballerina at the fancy dress competition.*

One of the nuns had spent hours curling my hair with tissue paper and rags. I was very pleased with the results.

*Me at Boarding School
as a stick of celery, sitting next to the gardener in our school play.*

I was originally given the lead role of 'Baby Onion', but had to speak with a squeaky, high-pitched voice for the part, which I refused to do as I thought that was very silly. So, my part was given to someone else. A lesson for the future, I wonder?

Sketch:

A White Christmas

(The husband is either onstage sat reading a newspaper complete with flat cap and slippers, or offstage and shouted to from time to time)

Mrs White: Christmas! The housewife's nightmare. 'Christmas comes but once a year', they say, well thank God for that at least or I'd never cope. Oh, no – more post! Well let's hope it's from someone I've sent one to this time. (*reads it*) 'Wishing you a happy Christmas and a prosperous New Year, love from George and Irene.' Oh, isn't that nice. (*to husband*). It's from George and Irene. George and Irene! We haven't sent them one. I must put them on me list under 'G' for George – 'cards'. Then there's old Mrs Smith. No, she didn't send us one last year and we sent her one. She can come off my list for a start, and so can Mrs Hunt now I come to think of it. She didn't send us one either. You soon find out who your friends are at Christmas time that's for sure.

Presents. I must make sure I don't send Jenny the soap she sent us last year. (*Looks at list*) No, she sent us the bath salts, and Mary sent us the soap – so I'll send Mary the bath salts and Jenny the soap. Any more unwanted gifts. Oh yes! (*Takes a scarf out of the box*) Who on earth sent me this, I wouldn't be seen dead in it! Oh yes. I remember. That girl's got no taste. No taste at all. I know I'll give it to Edith.

(*Starts to decorate the tree and sings verse 1 of 'It came upon a midnight clear'*) Peace on the earth, goodwill to men. You must be joking. You should have seen them in the supermarket last week pushing and shoving to get that last jar of mincemeat. Gladys got it in the end, and then someone pushed her, accidental on purpose like, and she dropped it. That soon wiped the smile off her face double quick, I can tell you!

What's this doing in here? (*fishes a piece of mistletoe out of the box*) I'm not having our Joe and that Carol smooching under it again like last year. And the thought of 'im (*gestures to where the husband is*) with a silly grin on his face saying, 'Happy Christmas luv,' is more than I can stand. I know where that can go (*throws it in the bin*) – best place for it. Christmas! There's always so much to do what with the cards and the presents, the food and the decorations (*indicating the husband*)... and of course 'e does nothing as usual. Leaves everything to me. It's always the same.

What's it all about, eh, Christmas? You know I used to love Christmas when the kids were young. It was magical. There's no other word for it but magical. You should have seen the kids' faces when they saw Mary and Joseph and Jesus lying in a manger, and the Wise Men and the shepherds. Our Joe used to say that Christmas was Jesus' birthday and that the Christmas cake was Jesus' birthday cake. He wanted us to put one thousand, nine hundred and something candles on it. That's kids for you. But we 'ad one, after all at Christmas Jesus was only a baby, wasn't He? It's a good job the neighbours went away every year 'cos I don't know what they would have thought if they'd heard us singing 'Happy birthday to You, happy birthday to You, happy birthday dear Jesus, happy birthday to You'. (*to husband*) Look, it's snowing. I always like it when there's a bit of snow. It's so Christmassy somehow.

You know, I used to love Christmas when I was a lass. I couldn't wait to go down to the church at the end of our street to see the crib scene with the Baby Jesus lying in the manger. I used to close me eyes and pray, and I always thought that when I opened my eyes, He would be there smiling up at me. It never happened of course. Well, I mean they were only statues after all, weren't they? (*gets out the nativity set*) Eh, I wonder what she were really like, Mary? I wonder how she felt at being chosen to be the mother of God. I bet she were right proud, I know I would be. I wonder how she felt when the Angel Gabriel appeared to her at the 'Annunciation'. That's what it's called you know. I know because I had to play the Angel Gabriel in the school play. I had to wear some silver tinsel in my hair. (*re-enacts the scene*) 'Fear not, for the Holy Ghost will overshadow you and the Child that will be born of you will be the Son of the Most High God.' That's what I had to say. 'Fear not'. I really wanted to be Mary. I wonder what she was like? The real Mary, I mean, not Susan Slattersly, who was chose to play the part. She was always teacher's favourite, and she had long blonde hair. I wonder if people believed her when she told them of the Angel appearing to her. The real Mary, I mean, not Susan Slattersly. I wouldn't have believed her – well would you? I mean what if our Elsie's lass came up with a tale like that? I certainly wouldn't believe her. I know we believe Mary, now, after all these years, but that's only because we know the whole story. You know, the miracles, and Easter and stuff. Eh, poor Mary.

(*Gets out more nativity figures*) To think at one time, Christmas was happening for the very first time and all these were real people just like you and me. The shepherds and the Wise Men and Mary and Joseph and the Angel, that's if you can call an Angel a real person that is! And now they make models, statues of them. It makes you think doesn't it? (*looks at the statue of the Baby Jesus and sings*) 'Oh holy Child of Bethlehem descend to us we pray, cast out our sin and enter in be born in us today. We hear the Christmas angels their great glad tidings tell. Oh come to us, abide with us our Lord Emanuel'. (*She put it with the rest and then says to husband.*) Happy Christmas, luv. (*If husband is on stage, she gets the mistletoe out of the bin before going over to give him a kiss and then says, 'Happy Christmas, luv'*).

Song:

Gift

Words by Linda Mae

Music by Anna Appleyard

What gift shall I give

What gift have I here?

What gift shall I give

To Jesus so dear?

If a rich man I, I would give some gold

Some jewels, some silver

Precious stones untold.

What gift shall I give

What gift have I here?

What gift shall I give

To Jesus so dear

If a poor man, I

I would give my skill

I have no gold, no gifts

And yet I will –

Give to Him my heart

Give to him my home

Give to Him my worship – to Him alone.

Sketch:

Shirley

(She is sat holding a teddy bear that is old and scruffy – hers from childhood.)

What's it all about eh, life? You know – you live – you die. (*to Teddy*) Not you of course... You're born... You live... You die – so what?

Every day it's the same – you get up, eat breakfast, go to work – if you're lucky enough to have a job that is. Then you come home, have yer tea – watch telly, go to the pub, stagger back, go to bed, and then next morning, it starts all over again. Get up, go to work, have yer tea, watch telly, go to the pub, stagger back, go to bed, get up. And that's it, or that's how it seems to me.

Life? God! You know I always thought there'd be something more to life. That one day something would happen. Oh I don't know what exactly. Um I'd become rich and famous or, er, I'd be discovered and end up on the telly watched by millions of viewers every week in the latest soap or, er, I'd fall madly in love and live happily ever after. Some hope! (*to Teddy*) I mean look at me. Reduced to talking to a – to a stuffed toy!

'And they all lived happily ever after.' And we swallow the whole concept. I blame the romantic novels meself and the films. Roses round the door. Champagne for breakfast! Life's just not like that!

Fairy stories. Do you remember them? Prince meets peasant girl (who just happens to be a Princess). Princess kisses a frog who turns into a handsome Prince 'and they all lived happily ever after' and we believed it or half believed it – why because we wanted to. We wanted there to be more to life. We still want there to be more. More than the 9 – 5 job, the mortgage – the boring round of events. More than christenings – weddings – funerals. Something in us cries out, screams out for there to be more. God!

I remember when I was five I thought there was more. I hoped there was more. I needed there to be more. I needed to know that somebody loved me... That somebody cared. That God loved me. I knew me dad didn't. I knew me mum didn't. I knew me step-mum couldn't. (*sings*) Where is love? Does it come from skies above lalalalalaaa…?

I remember walking into a dark dining room in a strange house one day. There was a dog Jeff. A Bull Mastiff. He loved me. He licked me face overjoyed to find a friend. Nearly knocking me flying. He used to let me ride on his back. Let me talk to him (*to Teddy*) like you're doing now. My friend Jeff!

I remember going into a school hall soon after. Away from Jeff. Away from home. There were girls playing. Boarders. I was made to join them. Dad left. I was alone with strangers. There was no one my age. No boarders aged 5. And I was a long way from home.

'God loves you' the nuns said. They were Roman Catholic. French. 'God loves you and He sent His Only Son Jesus to die on the cross for your sins,' they said. 'Jesus has gone back into Heaven to prepare a place, a home for you and for all those who love Him and trust Him,' they said. 'He will be your Friend for life. He will never leave you or forsake you'

I wonder?

Chapter 7

Words

'Sticks and stones may break my bones, but words can never hurt me!' Who on earth wrote such a saying? Absolute rubbish! I would imagine that more people are scarred for life by careless, thoughtless, or vindictive words than by any physical attack or accident.

'You're stupid,' 'you're clumsy,' 'you'll never hold down a job,' 'you'll never have any friends,' 'you'll end up in trouble with the police,' 'no one will want to marry you.' Sound familiar? Such words were said to me, too, in the past, and unfortunately, I took many of them into my spirit where they festered, and still cause havoc from time to time. Many of them however were discarded when a voice inside me at the outset said, 'that's not right, that's rubbish!

Thank God for positive input to balance such words, and heal. It took my husband ten years of telling me he loved me before I started to believe that such a thing was possible! My response used to be, 'You can't. What is there for you to love about me? I'm not worth it. How sad this must have made my Heavenly Father, and my husband for that matter.

At one point in my life I was on anti-depressants, sleeping pills, etc., and my dad said, 'I wish you didn't take those. I don't like to see you like this.' That was enough to make me throw them away immediately, and I believe it was the last time I needed any for several years, and all because someone cared enough to pass comment. While I was living at the YWCA shortly after leaving home at seventeen, I stopped eating. It got to such a state that whenever I did have any food I was sick. One day my roommate said, 'Please eat something even if it's only soup. I can't bear to see you killing yourself.' From that day, I started to eat again very gradually and the problem has never reoccurred.

At one time, the doctors sent me to see a psychiatrist. I had several sessions talking to him and he decided to give me some E.C.G treatment. What happens is that electric shocks are sent into the brain to wipe out some of the memories. As the day drew near, I became less and less certain about this, so I prayed. On the day the treatment was meant to commence, the man turned to me suddenly and said, 'You don't need this. You have a strength in you that is stronger than any of this. Use it.' And with that, I left, never to return. Did he know the 'strength' was my faith? I have often wondered. I do hope so.

While at Teachers' Training College in York, I was in a terrible state. I remember thinking what a disappointment I must be to God. Here was His 'ambassador' struggling just to get through each day emotionally and physically. What a dreadful witness I must be. Surely, nobody who knew me would want to become a Christian after meeting me? This was in the days of enthusiastic Christian Union members trying to convert the whole college single-handed, and coming to your room if you were ill and praying for your healing. You almost felt pressured into getting up and 'being well' even if you still felt really ill. Well, you were told that if their prayer didn't heal you immediately, it was because of your lack of faith! Or worse still, that you must have some unconfessed sin in your life. This of course put you on a guilt trip as you tried to work out what on earth you were doing that was so wrong.

It was at this time of feeling so unworthy as a Christian witness that a non-Christian sought me out saying that she would like the faith that I had, and how could she become a Christian? To this I replied that she should go and see Melvyn, our church youth leader, and he would tell her how she could become a Christian. How ridiculous – when I knew at the age of five exactly what to do.' Thankfully Carol went to see him and is still a Christian today despite many trials and tribulations in her life. At one point I asked her why she had come to me? She told me that she could see that I was a Christian 'despite' all the things I had been through, and that that was what had encouraged her. I was more used to the school of thought that said that you were a Christian because you couldn't cope with life, and that religion was a crutch, so this was a refreshing change – and much nearer the truth.

Sketch:

Noah

(Enter Mrs Noah with a sweeping brush)

MRS NOAH: Noah, Noah. Where is the man? Noah! A laughing stock that's what we'll be. He wants to build a boat. Here. In the middle of the desert. Hundreds of miles from the nearest sea. Says God told him to. Says the world's about to be flooded. Flooded! We haven't had a drop of rain in months.

He'll be out there now collecting more wood. He's been doing it for weeks and I won't be able to keep it a secret much longer. I'm having trouble hiding all the wood as it is. The neighbours are already asking questions and I'm running out of excuses. Tables, chairs, cupboards, go-carts – there's only so much you can make out of wood you know.

And that's not all. Oh, you haven't heard the best bit yet. When the boat, the Ark as he calls it, is built, we have to collect two of every animal, or so he says and take them into the Ark with us. Well, I mean, can you imagine it? He says God has told him! If you ask me, our Noah has been out in the sun too long... it's gone to his head. God told him indeed. We'll soon see about that. I'll be telling him a few things myself if he's not very careful!

Out there in the sun he is, all hours – praying. He says God talks to him. All he does is pray, pray, pray. Talking to God, he calls it. Well I can't really imagine God wanting to talk to our Noah, can you? I mean, I find it hard enough and I'm married to him!

He says God tells him what to do. Well is that normal, I ask you? A man of his age should take things easy, slow down. Not go imagining things, thinking God's talking to him all the time. Spending his days collecting bits of wood.

No, it's got to stop. I mean he's already thinking of chasing after wild animals. I'm just worried in case he might actually catch some. The odd tortoise or snail for example! But seriously, what does he think he's doing? If he manages to catch anything, anything at all, does he really expect it, sorry, I mean them, to stand in a queue waiting… waiting for the flood?

I can just imagine it, can't you? Two of everything. Two lions. Two lambs. A lion lying down with a lamb, whoever heard of such a thing? It'd be lamb chops that night all right. And what about the cats and the dogs chasing each other round in ever decreasing circles! It doesn't bear thinking about. And the noise – barking, howling, hissing, meowing… and that's just the cats and dogs.

What about when we've got the ants and the antelopes, the bats and the bears, the chickens and the cheetahs, the dogs and the dingoes, the elephants and the eels, the frogs and the ferrets, the goats and the geese, the hippos and the hyenas, the ibex and the iguanas, the jackals and the jackdaws, the kangaroos and koalas, the leopards and the lamas, the mongeese and the monkeys, the newts and the gnats, the octopus and the orang-utans, the peacocks and the pheasants, the quails, the rats, the rodents, the snakes, the spiders, the tigers, the tarantulas, unicorns, vixen, wildebeeste, yak, zebras – the complete A to Z of all creatures… all in our Ark. (*Sound of hammering*)

Noah, I don't believe it. He's started to build the Ark. What will the neighbours say? Noah! What's that you say? I can't hear you for all that noise. I can't hear you above all the hammering. You want me to fetch our sons to help. They're to come with us. God says? And their wives? Noah you've got to be joking. The animals are one thing but... Noah? Men – I give up. (*Exits*)

Sketch:

Ointment

Some of the words in brackets can either be spoken or can become stage directions. The woman enters carrying the vial of ointment.

Woman: The perfume spilled all over His feet filling the whole room with it's fragrance. For a moment everything stopped. There was a silence, a stunned silence as they surveyed the scene.

I had run into the room a few minutes earlier and thrown myself down at Jesus feet, weeping. I'd heard all about Him, followed at a distance. Seen His miracles of healing. The blind seeing, the lame walking, the deaf hearing, demons cast out, sins forgiven.

I saw that He was a friend of the people, the common people. I saw that at a glance. He wined and dined with publicans and sinners. Met people at the point of their need. He infuriated the religious, the self-righteous though. Their lack of compassion, their darkness was seen clearly in His light. He called them a brood of vipers, whited sepulchres. But for the little child, the poor, the widow He had nothing but love and compassion healing and restoring them.

I hadn't planned to do what I did. It was not premeditated. It's just that I had heard that Jesus was dining at Simon the leper's house that night.

I sat alone in my room thinking, imagining what it would be like to be there with Jesus – to be one of the chosen at the feast. Greeted with a kiss, my head anointed with oil as an honoured guest. My feet ceremonially washed.

I put on my best clothes, prepared myself, pretended that I had been invited... No one would even give me the time of day. Women would turn away from me in the street, shun me. And if their husbands dared to look in my direction they were quickly ushered away, protected. After all, I was a woman of ill repute! And yet, those same men their husbands, and others, who looked down on me in the light of day, were the ones who would come crawling to my house when all was dark and hidden.

It made me sick. They were no different from me. Worse in fact. I was only trying to earn a living. What was their excuse? A sudden crash jarred my thoughts as a stone flew through my window shattering my dreams.

Men: *(A group of them slightly drunk – we hear their voices only)* Whore. Filthy whore. How much longer do you expect us to stand out here waiting, you slut? *(etc., ad lib. They hammer at the door)*

Woman: What a life I had led. The lies, the degradation. If only I could start all over again, do things differently, clear my muddied reputation. If only...

Men: *(start hammering at the door again)* Open up, open the door, you slut! Open up now or you'll regret it you whore. *(etc., ad lib)*

Woman: I grabbed the vial of perfumed oil that I had been saving, and while the men were distracted, I ran barefoot out of the back of the house and along the narrow streets to Simon's house. I had no idea how I would get in but with all the noise and music, no one saw me enter. I looked around the room and there, in a corner, surrounded by His disciples was Jesus. *(Before anyone could stop me, I threw myself down at His feet weeping bitterly, my sobs drowning all other sounds as I handed my breaking heart over to Him.)*

(There was a stunned silence, followed by an explosion from Judas. Indignation, greed, jealousy – who knows what? He grabbed me and tried to throw me out, but Jesus stopped him. Then he turned and challenged his Master.) (Judas snatches the vial of ointment from her.)

Judas: That ointment could have been sold for a great deal, and the money given to the poor! *(Jesus takes it off Judas and gives it back to her)*

Jesus: The poor will always be with you but I will not always be here.

Simon: *(to audience)* This man calls Himself a prophet, but He doesn't even know what sort of woman she is!

Woman: Jesus knew all right. That's what makes it so amazing. He stood up for me in front of them all. 'Do not try and stop her Judas,' He said, 'for she has done well. She has anointed me for my burial.' Then He challenged Simon saying, 'I came into your house and you did not wash My feet, but she has washed them with her tears. You did not give me the customary kiss of greeting, but she has not stopped kissing my feet, you did not anoint My head with oil, but she has anointed My feet with ointment. Therefore, her sins, which are many, are forgiven her. Then came the words I will never forget.

Jesus: Woman, your sins are forgiven you. Woman, your sins are forgiven you.

Woman: Then He said, 'Wherever the gospel is preached in the whole world, this story will be told in memory of her' – and He was talking about me!

Chapter 8

Colour and All That Jazz

I love colour. When I was first married I painted the living room 'nanook', a bright turquoise, the dining room bright orange, and the kitchen a cerise pink. It was the first time I had been let loose to be myself. Recently I have tried to be a bit more conventional and subdued. I allow myself one room for the colours I really love. At present this is the bathroom which has buttercup yellow painted walls with a grey shower suite, basin and toilet, and pillar box red curtains and a wicker chair with a pillar box red cushion, plus a vase of red roses. Recently the red curtains have been changed to purple ones and the shower has a purple shower curtain. The red cushion has gone but the red roses remain. My eyes just feast on colour!

It never ceases to amaze me how as Christians we are almost made to feel guilty for liking vibrant colours as if they were somehow 'evil' or 'worldly'. It reminds me of the time I told a lady that I was going to drama school. Shocked she informed me that I was entering the devil's territory. 'Hallelujah' – someone needs to. After all, we are meant to be salt and light in the world, aren't we? And we are meant to be who we are meant to be. 'For freedom Christ has set us free' the Bible says – so why is it that 'the Church' and Christians like to spend their time enslaving us. Friends and relatives also often try to do the same.

I wish I could get married all over again. To the same man, I hasten to add! I seem to have been conditioned all my life, like

Pavlov's dogs, to please. I realise of course that it was the constant desire for acceptance that often caused me to behave in such a way. Everything, apart from the flowers, roses from Andrew's garden, the playing of the music 'Whiter Shade of Pale' by Procal Haram on the organ, and the hymn 'Take My Life And Let It Be', was chosen with other people in mind. What would they want me to wear? What would they want me to do? What is acceptable? Consequently, I hated my wedding dress. Only when it was cut up and made into a christening gown did I like it. Now in dress and in other ways I am learning to be myself and not to apologise for this. A friend recently said to me about themselves, 'It's O.K if people don't like my work as an 'artist' (he is a performer/singer/song writer). They have the freedom to not like it. It doesn't matter.' What a burden that lifted from me. I had always equated people not liking my work with not liking me!

At certain points in my life, it was easier if I felt that I was not liked or accepted, as I knew how to deal with that. After I hadn't heard from my father for years – I think it was about one Christmas card in ten years – I put him out of my mind, literally, so much so that when someone once asked me if I had a dad I said, 'No', and it was quite a shock to realise that in fact, I had. When I was at college and used to visit my best friends mother-in-law with her, I was in a dilemma. I didn't want to let my friend down, but I could hardly bear to stay. Mrs 'V', as everyone calls her, was just so kind. I used to sit at the end of the sofa nearest the door in case it got too much and I had to run out. She always made you a cup of tea and gave you a piece of cake or a chocolate biscuit, and was genuinely pleased to see you. It took me years to get used to it, but now every time we visit York, Mr & Mrs 'V' are our first port of call. She refers to me as 'the daughter she never had' and is as pleased to see me and my family as she was to see me all those years ago.

It was quite a surprise a few years ago to realise that I felt closer to God in a pub listening to jazz than in the church. Surely there must be something wrong with me. This could not be right? But it was, I mean is, a fact. Looking at colours, listening to jazz, going for a country walk, looking at an old building, even seeing beauty in a rubbish tip makes me feel close to my Creator, often closer than being in church 'doing all the right things'. I suppose I've always been a non-Conformist; I can't stand 'show' and 'pretence'. I would rather be 'honestly' wrong and 'do my own thing', than do what is expected, and then find out that this was not the way I should go. I can take full responsibility for my own mistakes, but not for those done while trying to be what others think I should be, and to do what others think I should do. For me, it is definitely a case of 'to thine own self be true'.

My wedding to Andrew on August 19th 1972 at St. Barnabas Church, York. My half-sister is the young bridesmaid. Sarah is now a professional musician and teacher.

Sketch:

Martha and Mary

Mary: We were like chalk and cheese, Martha and I. We couldn't have been more different? We never got on even as kids. Luckily for us, our brother Lazarus was always there to patch things up whenever we fell out. Poor old Lazarus, always trying to keep the peace, to mediate between us.

We both loved Lazarus. That was the one thing on which we did agree. And now he's gone. We sent for Jesus straight away. He was only in Jerusalem a few miles away. We thought that He would come immediately. He loved Lazarus. Everyone did. But three days had gone and still he hadn't come. We thought He would drop everything!

Jesus often came to our house. He was our close friend. Whenever He was in Bethany, He came to stay. It always put Martha in a flat spin. Everything had to be perfect you see. She was up at the crack of dawn cooking, cleaning, scrubbing, scouring – and of course we all had to join in. We usually managed to get it all done in time... But the last time Jesus came. I'm sure you can picture it. Martha fussing around as usual, panicking – driving us all insane.

When Jesus arrived, He didn't even seem to notice the mess. He sat down and started talking to Lazarus. Opening the scriptures, explaining. I couldn't help myself. I just had to join in. I curled up at His feet listening, drinking it all in. You would think I had committed an unforgivable sin to hear Martha carrying on! She came striding in, fuming – demanding that Jesus tell me to help her with the chores. 'Master,' she said, 'does it mean nothing to you that I am doing all the work by myself while Mary just sits here. Tell her to come and help me.' But He did no such thing. He turned to Martha and told her not to be so concerned about such things, saying that what I was doing was far more important and would not be taken away from me.

Our petty squabbles, our disagreements; the housework all seem so unimportant now. Now that our brother is dead. Why didn't Jesus come? If only He had been here, our brother would not have died. Even now, I'm sure that He could raise him from the dead. He could restore him to us. There is nothing that He cannot do!

I've seen Him open the eyes of the blind, cause the deaf to hear, the lame to walk. If only He had come then everything would have been all right.

Martha: When I heard that Jesus was here in Bethany, I ran out to meet Him, me – Martha. Mary stayed at home. It was me who greeted Him. 'Master,' I said, 'if You had been here, my brother would not have died. But I know that even now God will give You whatever You ask.' He told me that my brother would rise again, but I already knew that. 'Master,' I said, 'I know that he will rise again at the resurrection on the last day.' Then Jesus said to me, 'Martha, I am the resurrection and the life. He who believes in Me will live, even though he dies; and whoever lives and believes in Me will never die.' Could He really be saying that He was going to raise our brother from the dead, now? Right now, in front of our very eyes? I ran to fetch Mary, she always to understand Him better than me. It's always been the same. I used to be jealous of her if the truth be known. I was always practical one, the one who got things done while Mary, well, she was a dreamer. No help at all when things needed doing. I quickly told her that the Master had asked for her, and before I could say any more, she had run out of the house to meet Him. I ran after her. When she reached Jesus, she threw herself down at His feet. 'Lord,' she said, 'If You had been here my brother would not have died.' My exact words! Perhaps we're not so different after all. Jesus then asked us where the body had been laid. 'Come and see,' we shouted in chorus. It was then that we both stopped in our tracks. Jesus stood there weeping. Weeping over the death of our brother, and we had been wondering whether He even cared! He had only been in Jerusalem two miles away when we first sent the message and it had taken Him so long to arrive. All those with us could see for themselves just how much He loved Lazarus. Some still criticised Him though, saying that couldn't He who opened the eyes of the blind have stopped Lazarus dying, and I hate to admit it, but Mary and I had both thought exactly the same thing ourselves! When we reached the tomb, I thought Jesus was going to weep again. He was so moved that I felt ashamed of myself. He commanded that the stone be taken away. Before I could stop myself, I exclaimed, 'But Lord the body has been in the grave four days now and by this time it will stink!' Jesus rebuked me saying, 'Did I not tell you that if you believed you would see the glory of God?' And with that they took away the stone. Jesus stood outside the tomb. Everyone waited with bated breath to see what He would do. He prayed to His Father and then shouted with a voice loud enough to wake the dead, 'Lazarus come out!' What happened next is hard to describe. Suffice it to say, Lazarus came walking out of the tomb bound in his grave clothes. His hands and feet wrapped in strips of cloth; his face covered. 'Take off the grave clothes and let him go,' Jesus commanded, and then He restored him to us. His tears – were they because of our unbelief? Mary believes so, and looking back now – so do I.

Sketch:

The Woman at the Well (The Samaritan Woman)

She wears a leopard skin coat and a short skirt, is pregnant and looks very common. Calls to a group of people in the audience and waves to them.

WOMAN:

Hello! Coo-ee. Hello! You, yes you. I'm talking to you. I've just got to tell you. I've just got to tell everyone. I met this Man, you see. No, it's not what you think! I met this Man and He told me everything I've ever done. A stranger, too – not from round here. But He knew it all. He did. He told me everything. Bit embarrassing like. But He knew about Luke and Matt and John and Simon and Zacc, and He even knew about Ben!

Well, my first thought was that my 'ex' had been paying Him to spy on me. The usual. Collecting the evidence that sort of thing. God knows why. It wasn't as if we were ever married or anything. Legally, I mean. It was a sort of fatal attraction that drew us together, if you know what I mean. Couldn't keep our hands off each other. Very physical. But nothing else. Well, of course, the novelty soon wore off – well it does, doesn't it? His eyes started wandering – and I mean wandering. Well, one day I'd had enough. Two can play at this game, I thought. So, I went off with his best mate. That'll teach him, I thought. But he decided to teach me a lesson he said I'd never forget. Gave me a good hiding all right. Still got a couple of broken ribs to show for it. Seems like there was one rule for him and another for me. Well there always is, isn't there? Well, that was my first experience of 'true love'. Lasted all of five weeks as I remember.

Did a little better with his mate. Couple of months, as I recall. He was a different kettle of fish. Much quieter. A bit less rough round the edges, if you know what I mean. Quite a nice chap really. Oh, they do exist somewhere along the line from time to time. But he suddenly started staying away from home. Can't stand being ignored, me – so in the end, I looked elsewhere. It's not difficult, you know. Men are always on the lookout. Bit of make-up. Skirt an inch higher and it's a walkover. Looking back now, though, I think my 'ex' had warned him off, and being his mate, he knew exactly where to find him. Nasty temper my 'ex'. Nasty piece of work altogether. Can't see what I ever saw in him.

John was next. Yes, that's right. Yes, it was John. Charming man. Gift of the gab – everyone's friend. Thought I'd landed on my feet here, I did. 'Til I found out how he got his money. Selling young girls, that's what he did. He would chat them up. Buy them presents. Get their trust. Then he'd say that he'd got them a real good job. He would be their manager etc., etc. But they weren't to tell no one about it. Surprise them, he would say, by bringing home your first pay packet. Trouble is, they were never seen again. Well, I didn't want to get mixed up in anything like that. So I left – and he didn't even try to stop me!

Simon was next. Thought I'd try the older, more mature man. Get some respect. Get looked after for a change. Shows how much I know. Very possessive was our Simon. Used to lock me in whenever he went out. Didn't want me to talk to no one, or see no one. Locked me in whenever he couldn't keep his eye on me. Trouble is, he was always away on long business trips. Well, after the first two or three times, I got wise and planned my escape. He was furious. But as he'd already found someone else by then, he let it pass, so I was lucky. That was real narrow escape, I can tell you.

Zacc was OK. Nice guy. Wanted to settle down. Have a family. Have a family – me! You must be joking. Stayed with him a few months. No reason not to. But he got a bit heavy after that, wanting kids and commitment, that sort of thing. Not my style. So, that was that. Shame really. *(Counts on fingers)* Luke, Matt, John, Simon, Zacc – oh yes, He even knew about whatsisname. My one-night stand a couple of years back. Told me his name – 'Ben'. I'd forgotten all about Ben, till He said. That's how much it meant. A few minutes comfort, or, if I'm really honest – lust, and that was that. Oh, he wanted to see me again, did our Ben. But when I saw him in the light of the day, when I was no longer drunk, quite honestly I just wasn't that interested even though I was between blokes at the time. Then a few months ago, I got together with Zacc. We moved to a new spot, pretended to be a happily married couple, did and said all the right things. Zacc kept pestering me, so in the end I said I'd give it another go as long as he didn't hassle me about kids and he agreed. I thought we might actually make a go at it. That I might settle down. Well, miracles do happen!

Well, this Man, this stranger, asked me for a drink of water from the well. Well, you could have knocked me down with feather. Him, a religious bloke, a Jew, asking me for a drink. The Jews have nothing to do with us Samaritans. After all, we're the scum of the earth. And for Him, a Man, to talk to me, a woman, well, it was unheard of. Well, I just stood there. I mean, what if this was a wind-up? Jews don't go round asking anything of us Samaritans. Then He said that if I knew who it was who was asking me to get Him a drink, I would ask Him to give ME a drink and He would give me living water. Well, I wasn't going to take this lying down. 'Sir,' I said, 'you haven't even got a bucket to get the water with. Do you think you're greater than our ancestor Jacob who gave us this well and drank from it himself along with his sons and his herds?' Then He said that whoever drinks of the water in this well will thirst again, but whoever drinks of the water that He gives, will never thirst again. 'The water that I will give will spring up inside him bringing him eternal life,' He said.

Well, I didn't know anything about eternal life, but I did know that I was sick and tired of drawing water from the well every day, and anyway, what was with all this 'him'. Whoever drinks the water I will give HIM – it will well up inside HIM giving HIM eternal life! 'Sir,' I said, 'give ME this water so that I won't thirst again. 'His reply was unexpected to say the least. He told me to go and fetch my husband and bring him back with me. Well, before I knew what I was doing, I blurted out the truth – 'Sir, I have no husband.' 'You are right,' He said, 'You have had five husbands and the one you now have is not even your husband!' 'You must be a prophet, a man of God to know all this,' I said. Then I decided to change the subject real quick. 'Our fathers worshipped on this mountain, Sir, but you Jews say that the place where we must worship is in Jerusalem.' 'Believe me woman,' He said, 'a time is coming when you will worship the Father neither on this mountain nor in Jerusalem. You Samaritans worship what you do not know, whereas we Jews worship what we do know for Salvation comes from the Jews. A time is coming and is already here when those that worship God will worship Him in spirit and in truth, for God is Spirit and those who worship Him must worship Him in spirit and in truth.' 'I have heard that the Messiah, the Christ, is coming and that when He comes, He will lead us into all truth,' I said. 'I am He', He replied, 'I am Jesus of Nazareth, your Messiah.' So, He was the infamous Jesus of Nazareth, I should have guessed! It all made sense now. Even in Samaria, we had heard so much about Him. The sick being healed, demons cast out, sins forgiven. Just then, His disciples came back with some bread. You should have seen their faces. What's He doing talking to her? What's she doing talking to Him? But no one dared say a word. It was dead funny. Well, I kept Him talking a little bit longer, just to prove a point, that He, Jesus, the Messiah, was happy to talk to me, a despised Samaritan woman, and then I rushed off to get my husband – I mean my Zacc.

I got quite a reputation after that. I became known as 'that woman Jesus spoke to!' I told everyone about Him and most of the village came to believe that Jesus really was the Messiah, the Son of God. Oh, not because of me, they said. No – but because they had seen Him for themselves. Jesus came and stayed with us for a few days. As for Zacc and me, well, we're married now. Meeting Jesus was the best thing that ever happened to us. Oh, there's only one problem. If it's a boy, I can't call it Luke or Matt or John or Simon or Ben; so let's hope it's a girl, eh?

*As the Samaritan Woman at the Well
- in a sketch from 'A Woman's Touch'*

Photo: Martin Hughes

Chapter 9

Romania

Like so many others about ten years ago, I did 'my bit' for Romania visiting and performing at the orphanages with my theatre company. First of all though my husband and I went on an organised coach tour to 'spy out the land' feeling rather like Joshua and Caleb. This was just before all the intensive media coverage, and shortly after the death of Nicolae Ceausescu. We actually went on a ride on his private yacht that was by then a tourist attraction.

Would we be allowed into the orphanages? We were shown only one, which appeared to be their 'showcase' and were told that there were no others in the area, which of course was not true, but politically correct. The 'others' were rather as we expected them to be! We did perform in the 'showcase', as we had taken costumes just in case, but that was all.

What a holiday. We certainly were 'organised', so much so that when we were given a free day, we were at a loss to know what to do after so many days of being marched around looking at monasteries and monuments, and only going where we were told. We were on the coach being 'guided' from after breakfast until evening meal time each day. The food was the best they had, but suffice it to say there were always one or two in the party suffering from constipation or 'the runs', and everyone was popping pills!

When we planned the holiday, we took loads of gifts with us for 'whomever'. Lindy gave me one of her best dolls. A pretty one with long blonde plaits, dressed in a tartan dress. In one sense, she didn't really want to part with it, so she told me to make sure that I gave it to someone special.

One day, on a tram travelling to Bucharest, I only had very few presents left, a toilet roll and a bar of soap. I was sat next to an old man and I felt that I should give these things to him. The feeling was very strong, but I was afraid I might offend him. Well how many people have you given a present of a toilet roll to? I gave him the toilet roll. He took two pieces off the roll and handed it back to me. I gestured that he was to have the whole roll and then gave him the bar of soap for good measure. I was just sorry that I had no tracts left. We somehow wanted the people to know that we were giving to them because God loves them, but not speaking Romanian, there was nothing I could do. A few seconds later, he got off the tram and I was sat there wondering if I had done the right thing. I happened to glance out of the window and there was the man looking into his shopping bag with a smile on his face as though someone had given him the world.

Another day, we saw an old lady selling a few sunflower seeds in a jar. We had just stopped as a coach load at a hotel for lunch and now we were off to yet another monastery or church. As the coach turned out of the hotel drive, there was the woman. I said, 'Lord what is the point in showing her to us now that it is too late to give her anything?' You didn't ask Romanian guides and coach drivers to stop while you nipped out to talk to the locals! A minute or so later, we stopped. There was a monastery. Why they had driven us that short distance I'll never know. We were told we had fifteen minutes, or was it ten? We told one of our party what we were doing and, as the rest all went round the monastery, we raced back to the hotel to the lady. We gave her a Christian leaflet and a present. She couldn't understand us and we couldn't understand her, but that was good. Two businessmen came to help. We gave them a New Testament each, and when the lady's daughter arrived, we gave her a booklet and a present too. If we had been able to give our presents when we wanted, those men would not have got their New Testaments, and maybe the daughter would not have received her present. Instead of one, we ended up giving to four. We raced back and arrived at the coach just as our party was filing back on to it ready for our next destination.

Another time, the coach pulled up at the roadside where some men were selling watermelons. Again, the presents were running low. I had some razor blades and a gent's hanky, so I gave one to one man, and one to the other, again wishing I had some tracts left to let them know why we were doing this. To my amazement, they called me back and handed me the biggest watermelon imaginable. They didn't want paying for it; they just wanted to give. It reminded me of when we gave some presents to some children in a village. One handed me a wild flower, and another a walnut from a tree growing nearby. The walnut shell was empty – but it's the thought that counts, so they say, and it certainly was.

The doll was a real problem. Every day, after a quick 'arrow' prayer I would load the carrier bag with presents. Each time I went to put in the doll, it didn't seem right. It had to be given to someone special. In theory, that was fine, but we were running out of days. Then one day, a couple on our tour happened to mention that they were going to visit a poor family. Now, it seemed right to give them the doll plus many other things we had left. I even went round other members of the coach party asking them for a gift or some piece of their clothing for this family. I think Andrew, my husband, literally lost his shirt that day.

Our friends arrived back with an amazing story. There was a little girl of about five in the family. She had been born either deaf and dumb, or blind and deaf. She had a combination of two out of the three. Her family were Christians and often prayed for her. One day, when she was three, she was miraculously healed on the sofa in her own home. This girl had prayed that the next time a lady came from England, she would be brought a doll, and now my Lindy's doll was the answer to her prayer. Isn't Father God so good? That incident alone would have made the trip to Romania worthwhile. Too much else happened to write it all down.

At one monastery, I prayed that I could give a Bible to the right Priest (they did not usually have the Word of God. It was all tradition and religious teaching, and the Bible was viewed with suspicion; many would not have accepted one. Some of our party tried to give them Bibles, but the Bibles were rejected.) This one Priest, however, had caught my eye, and as I prayed, there just happened to be a few seconds when he was alone. I offered him a Bible, and he gratefully accepted. There was no awkwardness, no conniving – he was just there – the right person at the right time. Who knows what has happened in his life and others as a result of this meeting.

At one point, we were at a ski lift in Brannan Brasof and I prayed for the right people to give a Bible to. No one was around. Then these two locals appeared out of nowhere. I gave them the Bibles and then they were gone. Who knows who they were, and who knows why? Apart from God, that is.

My second visit to Romania was with an actor friend Andrew, as opposed to my husband, Andrew. The last time I had been part of an organised group and there was safety in this. Now there was just the two of us. Andrew had a very old rucksack and that was the root of our troubles. The fact that we had a load of costumes and props didn't help, nor did the numerous presents. The officials decided that the gunge in the straps of Andrew's rucksack was drugs – cocaine, who knows what? It was polystyrene, or something, that over the years had turned to powder! The officials tried burning it, placing it in alcohol, even tasting it. Our luggage was scrutinised. The 'Earl Grey' teabags were very suspect, as were the lavender bags lovingly sewn by friends. We were taken into a room, our passports confiscated, and guarded by sixteen-year-old soldiers armed with guns, as our luggage was inspected by officials increasingly higher in rank. I even began to wonder what the inside of a Romanian jail looked like. Andrew was taken into a room and body searched. One of the young soldiers wanted our little plastic snake that was a prop for 'Patchwork Quilt', the play about disability awareness that we were performing in the orphanages. If we gave it him, would we then be bribing him? Or should we say 'no' to someone holding a gun? We did say, 'No'. We had come for the children and this was an important prop. When I went to the loo, I was accompanied by a female soldier. At this point, I was beginning to question the sanity of trying to obey God's will!

When we were first 'arrested', if that is what was happening, and our passports taken off us, there was a cleaner, a man, leaning on his brush saying, 'It's plastic, it's plastic!' Why didn't they listen to him? He knew that Andrew was travelling with a very old rucksack and it was just plastic, or the equivalent, that was old and causing the powder effect. Hours later, we were released as they realised their mistake. Our friend picking us up had long since gone home hours ago, assuming that we had decided not to come after all. It was about 11pm; we were in a strange city and a strange country. I asked to be allowed to make one phone call. We called a cab and eventually arrived at our host's home to start our tour of the orphanages. The following year when I went with Martin, another actor friend, to perform in the orphanages, I made sure that there were no Earl Grey teabags, and definitely no *pot pourri* sachets. Even the soft toys were limited because the soldiers had considered slitting them open in case any drugs had been smuggled in them.

At one orphanage we visited, there were lots and lots of little boys ranging from seven to twelve years old, marching as if under a dictator regime. At the end of our performance, I went to give the gifts to them. They became like wild animals. I had to drop the bag that I was holding and let them fight it out between them. Every boy had a crew cut, and all were dressed in the same drab uniform. Soul destroying. No wonder they fought for the gifts. Not one of them had anything belonging to themselves. No one cared for them as individuals. They craved love. My only hope is that by some miracle they find it – God's love.

Sketch:

Mary at the Cross

Mary:

Jesus my Son. Hanging on the cross. At the crossroads of Your life, the crossroads of Your death. Why are you there? You could come down from the cross. You could save yourself. There is nothing that you cannot do. Remember the water into wine at the wedding feast at Cana. You chose to obey me then. Obey me now my Son and come down from the cross. Do not let them kill You – not like this! You stilled the storm on Lake Galilee. Still the storm in my breast, my Son. Release me from this torture of watching You die. 'Peace be still,' You said, and even the wind and the waves obeyed you. Peace be still.

How still you are my Son. At peace with your God. In pain and yet at peace. Bleeding and yet interceding. 'Father forgive them for they know not what they do.' How can You forgive at such a time as this? I could not. I would call down thunder and lightening to strike them, to show them that you are God incarnate. I look at You, my Son, Your back scourged and bleeding still. The nails in Your hands and feet, the crown of thorns on Your head. God in Heaven, why are You allowing this! This is Your beloved Son, Your chosen One in whom You are well pleased. Is this His reward for serving You…for obeying You, a God of Love? He gave You to me, this God of Love. 'A virgin will conceive and bear a Son.' And I obeyed. I accepted the responsibility wholeheartedly. Willingly. 'I am the handmaid of the Lord. Let it be done unto me according to Your will.' But not this. I cannot accept this.

'You shall bear a Son and you shall call His name Jesus for He shall save His people from their sins,' Gabriel announced, and I was happy. Happy to face misunderstanding for my Lord and my God. But I did not know what things I would have to face... What things You would... 'This Child is destined to cause the falling and rising of many in Israel, and to be a sign that will be spoken against so that the thoughts of many hearts will be revealed.' You were only eight days old, when Simeon told me this, 'and a sword will pierce your own soul, too'. You healed the sick. Because of You the blind can see, the lame can walk, the deaf can hear. You cast out demons, redeemed lives. Why are they treating You like this? The soldiers are casting lots for Your garments, laughing and swearing. Unaware of who You are – of Who it is they crucify. I cannot bear to see You more. To watch You suffer. Your disciples have deserted You. Even the sun refuses to shine. The whole of nature is in rebellion at this awful sight.

'Eloi, Eloi, lama sabachthani - My God, my God why have You forsaken me?'

Has the Father Himself deserted You, my Son? It is our sins that separate You from Your Father, my Son. He cannot bear to look on You as You take upon Yourself the sins of the world. 'Surely He hath borne our grief and carried our sorrows; yet we did esteem Him stricken, smitten of God and afflicted. But He was wounded for our transgressions. He was bruised for our iniquities: the chastisement of our peace was upon Him: and by His stripes we are healed.' 'It is finished!' Your suffering over. Your victory won. And still You are with me. You will not leave me or forsake me. I hear Your words, 'Peace be still' and know that all is well.

*As Mary at the Cross
- in a sketch from 'A Woman's Touch'*

Photo: Martin Hughes

Chapter 10

Healing

I was standing in a line at the front of the auditorium in York University along with many others. I watched as the preacher, an Anglican minister, the Reverend Trevor Dearing prayed for each person, laying hands on them as he did so. Some fell to the floor. Next to me on my left was a very big man at least six foot two and quite sturdy with it

'Lord, I know You heal people,' I prayed, 'but please don't let me get in the way by putting up my usual barriers or trying too hard. If You want to heal me today don't let me stop You.' And I remember half praying 'Lord, You know I've got a really bad neck. I don't think it would be a good idea for me to fall down; after all, I might hurt myself, but I suppose it's up to You.'

By this time, the man on my left was being prayed for, and to my horror, he was falling towards me. This is when being four foot ten inches is not very helpful. For some reason, I stretched out a finger and placed it on his back. Believe it or not, that stopped him falling any further in my direction. He appeared for those few seconds to be weightless. While all this was happening, and I was distracted from worrying about whether or not I would be healed, I found myself lying on the floor feeling completely at peace. Trevor, I assume, must have placed his hands an inch or so above my head while he prayed, which gets rid of the question did she fall (under the power of the Holy Spirit), or was she pushed!

I couldn't wait for my appointment to see the Consultant again. On the previous occasion, I had been falling asleep in the hospital waiting room with the pain. Members of the public, nurses and doctors kept coming up to me and asking if I was all right. This in itself was so unusual that I started to worry about how bad I really was. When I had the x-ray, it was almost impossible to lie correctly. For some reason, I had kept trapping nerves in my neck, about every five minutes it seemed! This was the time I was told that I had the spine of an eighty year old. Not very helpful when you have three young children and can't even dress yourself in the morning without help.

The children were all taken off me; the youngest two being taken every morning by my husband, to a nursery at the back of where he worked. I was given maximum help via the council from a cleaner each week. At the time, I couldn't even hold a potato to peel it, and holding a cup of tea to drink was extremely difficult. Unfortunately, the pain-killers didn't! I was amazed to find that modern medicine couldn't cope. I had the strongest doses allowed and it just made no difference.

Times like this certainly made sense of 1 Corinthians, chapter 12, 'For the body is not one member, but many. If one member suffer, all the members suffer with it.' I had one trapped nerve in my neck, but my fingers went numb, my whole body felt in pain, and the only place I could find a little comfort was sat on a bean bag that moulded itself to me. My wonderful Christian doctor said, 'Tough – you've got it for life,' or words to that effect!

Humanly speaking of course, he was right. My body had 'worn out', my spine was a disaster, and I was only in my twenties.

I had to wear one of those awful plastic collars all the time. Not one of the soft ones, which are bad enough, as anyone who has ever had to wear one can verify. I had to wear a plastic one which pushed your chin right up causing your neck to remain in a straight position, and went right down to your chest and had to be secured with leather straps. Very uncomfortable in hot weather. On leaving the healing meeting, I used it as an umbrella as it was raining!

I only went to the meeting because I had told a new friend about it and invited her for dinner saying that we would take her in our car, as she had no transport and could not have got there without us. I hate to let anyone down; it has happened to me too much in my life, so although I was in agony and could hardly move, I went.

The hospital had told me that they normally avoid operating on the neck, but because I was in such a bad state, the Consultant would do an emergency operation as soon as possible. When I went back and put my head round the door, he didn't even let me sit down, saying that if I ever needed him in the future I could make an appointment to see him!

I have received many such physical healings in my life, usually when the medical profession couldn't really help any more. Healing of memories and the healing of emotions, however, were quite another thing, often taking a great deal of time. Much of my healing has come via my husband and my children, and more recently, my grandchildren.

When my children were young, and now it works for my grandchildren, I used to say, 'Let me kiss it better.' Whether it was a bruised knee or a bang on the head, it seemed to make no difference. Love always worked. And so it is with emotional healing, their love and the love and acceptance of others cannot fail.

Sketch:

A Woman's Touch

I touched him. I crept forward in the crowd and touched Him. I'd tried everything else. Spent all my money on doctors and cures year after year. Each time grasping at straws. Each opportunity bringing hope for a fleeting moment, only to disappear into thin air. I used to have money, you know. But money can't buy everything. In my case, it couldn't buy me health.

There was nowhere left to turn. I was in despair. How much longer, how much longer could I stand the disgrace? It was not an illness you could talk about, you see, share with your friends. It was far too personal. Could not be talked about, only whispered in secret corners, and then only to a chosen few. Twelve years I had carried this burden and I could take it no longer. No more doctors for me, no more shattered dreams. No more dashed hopes. I had decided it had to end. There could be no turning back. Not this time. Oh, I'd heard about Jesus, of course, who hadn't? News travels fast. The blind being healed, the deaf, the dumb, the lame. Eyes opened, ears unstopped, tongues loosened, feet made to walk. But what was that to me. These stories of hope. After all, they always happened to someone else – they would never happen to me.

I set off not quite knowing where I would go. To my surprise, the sun was shining. Everywhere, people seemed in a holiday mood as they swarmed the crowded streets. I found myself being carried along by the crowd. I kept hearing the name

Jesus, Messiah, Rabbi, Master, but my heart was too full. The turmoil of my life. The pain. The suffering. Why? What had it all been for? The crowd suddenly came to a halt, and there straight ahead of me was Jesus. I found myself listening to His words. I edged forward pushing my way through the crowd. If only I could touch the hem of His garment then maybe I could be healed. If only I – if only I could touch the hem of His garment... if only I could touch the hem of His garment, surely I would be... I had done it. I had touched Him. Immediately the flow of blood stopped. I felt it. I felt it dry up within me. I felt whole and clean like a child again. Whole for the first time in years, in twelve years! The crowd started to move and I slipped back among them, unnoticed. I wanted to dance and shout and sing. I wanted to praise God, but I was too embarrassed, too ashamed. I would go home and thank Him later. No one ever need know.

"Who is it touched Me?" His voice rang out loud and clear.

My heart almost skipped a beat. His disciples were amazed. A jostling crowd and he asked who touched Him.

'Someone touched Me, for I felt power go out from Me.'

It was no good. I would have to admit it. I didn't know what I would say. I pushed my way back through the crowd and threw myself down at His feet.

He lifted up my head. 'Daughter,' He said 'Your faith has made you whole. Go in peace'.

And I did.

Sketch:

Eve

(Eve is an over the top theatrical actress dressed in evening dress, feather boa, jewels, etc.)

Eve, that's me darling. Mother of all sin. 'Did God really say?' the serpent hissed – and I doubted. Doubted our Father's love. Thought I knew best and paid the price.

You would think once would be enough wouldn't you sweetie, but still the serpent crawls around my life whispering his doubts. Curled, open fanged – waiting to devour, to lie... to cheat... to steal. Coiled and ready to strike. 'Did God really say? Did God REALLY say? You! You must be joking. He can't really love you now can He? Not after all you've done. He sent His Son to die for you? Don't make me laugh. Perhaps for a good man, one would dare to die... But you? Just look at yourself. Do you really think that God could love you?'

'He bore your sicknesses in His Body on the Tree. Then why all these aches and pains, why all these bouts of cold and 'flu'? You mustn't take things so literally, so seriously. You must face facts *(sssss).*' And back we go to the beginning.

'Eve - did God say that you could eat the fruit of every tree in the Garden?' 'Every tree but this one in the middle. If we eat the fruit of this tree we will surely die.' 'You'll not die God knows (*sssss*). If you eat the fruit of that tree, your eyes will be opened and you will become wise *(sssss)*. You will be like a god knowing good and evil.'

It sounded tempting enough and the fruit did look good to eat. What harm could there be? One little bite couldn't hurt now could it? And think of the knowledge I might gain. So, I ate the fruit – the forbidden fruit and so did Adam, and God forbid we became wise and the sweetness of the fruit became sour to our lips.

No fig leaves here, darling. I'm not in the Garden of Eden, nor ever have been. I'm Eve A.D. not B.C. I'm not the first, but neither will I be the last – Eve, I mean. I blame God, or was it Adam...I can't quite remember. But it was someone's fault. Man blames woman. Woman blames man. Everyone blames God and that's about the measure of it sweetie; that is if they admit God exists of course, which most people don't – until something goes wrong that is – earthquake, flood, famine, car accident, death, that sort of thing. And then it's all His fault. Oh. And then there's the snake, of course. The serpent. You can always blame him. Very handy that, then nothing is ever your fault!

Lucifer, angel of the morning, how are the mighty fallen indeed? 'How art thou fallen from Heaven, O Lucifer, son of the morning. How art thou cut down to the ground? For thou hast said in thy heart, I will ascend into Heaven. I will exalt my throne above the stars of God. I will ascend above the heights of the clouds. I will be like the most High.'

And with the same temptation you were tempted, you tempted us. An apple you used, a lousy apple, and our pride. And still you whisper your lies tempting us to unbelief – to doubt. 'Did God really say...?' Yet, you are a defeated foe. 'I will put enmity between you and the woman,' God said, 'and between thy seed and her seed. It shall bruise thy head, and thou shall bruise His heel.'

And so, as with Eve's disobedience, sin entered this world, so with Mary's obedience the way of salvation came 'Emmanuel - God with us.'

Chapter 11

More Healing

I am having trouble with my back. I can't sit, stand, lie down or walk without being in a great deal of pain. Once again, the painkillers don't work sufficiently. Although we haven't much money, I have spent £400 on a Swedish designer chair so that I can get some relief, and I have bought a 'backfriend' to carry round with me if I catch a bus or go to the theatre. It changes any seat into an 'orthopaedic' one and helps with the pain, and prevents you getting worse as it makes you sit correctly.

I think I blame 'men'. The designers of chairs over the years who do not cater for anyone much under five foot six. It's the same with the kitchen designs. Do they really expect us to reach those cupboards on the wall, except with a pair of stepladders! I refuse to have any wall cupboards in principle. I think the designers designed for themselves, thinking that if they could reach or sit down comfortably, so could everyone else. They should try years of sitting in a chair where their feet could not touch the ground and see what it does to their backs!

The doctor gave me sessions with the physiotherapist who worked from our doctor's surgery twice a week. What a character. I had never met him before. I walked in and sat down. He looked at me, looked at his notes and said – 'Hopeless case, dreadful posture, don't know what we can do here!' Did he talk to all his patients this way or was it just me? He then proceeded to 'insult' me in a friendly manner for the rest of the session, and every other time I attended which was once a week for several weeks, as well, of course, as manipulating my spine, muscles, etc. and giving me exercises to follow.

Thinking about it now, that's the way I talk to some of my one to one pupils, and the way that one particular very good friend of mine, Jonathan from the Birmingham Theatre School, used to talk to me. As long as you pick the 'right' person, and do it in the correct manner, it seems to do no end of good. Perhaps because there are not many people you can talk to in this manner, when you do they feel 'special'?

One day as I was sat there while the 'Physio' was perusing my notes, I prayed, 'Lord, please heal me so that this lovely man will know that You are still working in people's lives today,' and then promptly forgot about it! This was at the time the treatment that had been very beneficial had stopped working. I was doing everything correctly and yet things seemed to be showing no improvement, and were possibly getting worse. A couple of days before this I had prayed for the healing of my foot. I had been born with cerebral palsy. Sometimes, I could hide it especially on stage as I often wore long dresses 'in character'. But now I felt I wanted God to heal me.

On seeing a specialist years beforehand, we were told that to put things right, the heel cord in the right leg would need to be lengthened so that the heel could touch the floor. The very strong muscle on the inside of the foot which pulled it inwards would have to be switched with the outer one so that the foot could turn outwards, and work was needed to be done on my hip. However, as I was coping very well with the disability, they decided to leave well alone. That and the fact that if it went wrong I would end up in a worse state.

For years, people had been telling me to write and perform a play about Queen Esther, but I ignored it, for obvious reasons. Much later, I felt God telling me to do it. I even ignored this for a time, or at the very least, postponed it, as you do. Then, when it wouldn't go away, I came up with all the excuses under the sun. 'Lord, have you looked at me lately. I'm too old, not tall enough, not slim enough, I've got dark hair, and I've got a bad leg. Everyone knows that Esther was young, slim, beautiful and blonde. If You like, I'll write the play and be the narrator and get someone else to play the part of Esther.' Next came the 'fleeces' – well, I had to be absolutely sure!' 'I can't possibly play the part; I've no idea what she wore'. Attending a Jewish Messianic meeting in Nottingham, we were all handed a folded double A4 glossy leaflet. Inside was a photo of a commemorative doll of Queen Esther complete with costume. And that's not all. The doll was small in stature, had brown hair remarkably like mine, and a roundish face. It was like looking in the mirror. The eyes were brown, but that seemed to be the only difference.

I have never known anyone called Esther, but at this time of arguing with God, everywhere I went ladies were called Esther. I phoned a friend with a query, she said, 'Hang on a minute I'll just ask Esther.' (Esther was her cleaner who just happened to be there). I looked up at a shop sign – 'Esther'. I listened to a Bible reading – it was about 'Esther'. An article in a magazine, I read was on the life of 'Esther'. The daily Bible notes were on, you've guessed it, 'Esther'. By this time, I was beginning to weaken somewhat, but I still had my trump card.

'OK Lord, I'll do it, but my posture isn't very good and my foot turns in. I'll wear a long dress and pray that You hide my disability every time I perform, but it would be really good if you could heal my foot.'

This was on the Thursday, two days after I had prayed at the physiotherapists for my back to be healed. Once more, strangely enough, I then forgot all about it. A friend had asked me to go to a special Messianic concert in Nottingham with her and I agreed. She then said that she had arranged for us to stay over at a friend's house so that we could go to a little meeting held in a local school building on Shabbat. I felt a deep excitement at the prospect of going, like I had never felt before. We went on the train, me complete with backfriend. The Friday evening meeting where they had a famous, well-known, Jewish/ American singer was O.K, but to be truthful, I was rather bored. Being in pain didn't help. Everyone else clearly thought that he was brilliant, and no doubt, he was. It was here that I was handed the leaflet with the picture of Esther the minute I walked through the door. Unfortunately, I gave it to a friend who was originally going to make me the costume, and it has been lost. I would love to have been able to show the picture to you.

The next morning we went to the Messianic meeting. This is what I had really been looking forward to with so much anticipation, but I had no idea why. I think that there were about fifteen people there altogether, much less than usual. At the outset of the meeting, someone stood up and said that he believed that the Lord wanted to heal some people in the congregation, and would any of us like to come forward? Apparently, this was not the 'norm' at their meetings; in fact, I think this was a 'first'. And it wasn't the actual leader who had asked us to come forward. I went to the front with one or two others. There was no 'show' involved. I asked the man to pray for my back to be healed. To my surprise, he asked if he could pray for my legs instead, explaining that back problems are often caused by the difference in leg length. Then he asked me whether I wanted to be shorter or taller. Only a man could ask such a stupid question! At four foot ten, what would you say? I said, 'Taller please'. What I wanted to say was, 'I'd like to be five foot two with blonde hair, a stone lighter, and ten years younger please,' but I wasn't sure that he had a sense of humour, and perhaps this was not the time or the place. I was sat on a chair facing the front and closed my eyes, but was told to open them and watch what the Lord would do. I stretched both legs out in front of me as asked, and as I watched, the one leg grew in length to match the other. I was wearing black leggings at the time, and saw three definite 'ripples' go across the right leg, like a child drawing a wave of the sea, and I felt my bone, etc. extend, but it didn't hurt. While this was happening, I prayed that the Lord would strengthen and straighten my right foot 'while He was at it, and if He didn't mind'. This was for the sake of 'Hadassah', the play about Esther.

My back was healed, and my foot straightened. I had expected that when I went back to see Clive, my 'Physio', he would say, 'What must I do to be saved?' or words to that effect. Instead, he got me to touch my toes, get up on the couch, usually an impossibility, but this time I leapt on to it, and did various exercises. Eventually, I said, 'Have you noticed anything different about me today?' Annoying person, he must have known that I was dying for him to comment. I had told him that I had been prayed for and believed that my back was now OK, as soon as I had walked in. He admitted that he had seen a big difference. Said that he didn't need to see me again, but that he was always there if needed. I have not seen him since. Who knows what effect it all had on him? Maybe I'll never know.

As far as the straightening of the foot was concerned, I went home and had a 'ballet' exercise competition with my daughter, Anna. I think it was the 'third' position in ballet. The one where you have to make both feet stretch out to the side as far as possible. I won. Before this, my right foot would not even go straight let alone go out to the side as the lack of muscle strength had made this impossible, but that was before prayer!

For performing 'Hadassah', the first scene of which focuses on anti-Semitism, I now realise that I definitely needed the healing of my back. There is no way that I could have coped with the stage fighting without this. My posture also improved as a result of the healing, and this plus the straightening of the foot, made it so much easier to play a Queen. It is a powerful play, and very topical as anti-Semitism once again raises its ugly head.

Sketch:

The Woman Caught in Adultery

The woman is dragged up the aisle and thrown on stage.

Man: This woman was caught in the very act of adultery. Kill the whore. Stone her. Kill the harlot.

(The Scribe and Pharisee talk quietly together)

Man: *(impatiently)* Kill the harlot. *(Still no response)* Such a woman should be stoned to death. Moses' Law commands it. Whore. *(He spits at her)*

Woman: *(to audience)* I thought I'd heard footsteps but I put it out of my mind. It would be somebody going past to buy bread for the Passover. After all, I was always 'hearing' footsteps and they always went past. Besides no one knew we were here apart from Matt and I. I thought my mind was playing tricks on me as it had done a thousand times before. It must be the guilt. I'd always had a strong sense of right and wrong from as far back as I can remember. Even as a child I'd always tried to do what was right. What would please God?

I decided to try to forget about the footsteps - any footsteps. Then to my horror, they stopped and someone started hammering at the door. I held my breath and hoped they would go away. My heart was pounding. The hammering got louder and louder. It was then I realised what was happening.

Someone was trying to break in trying to break down the door. I looked around for somewhere to hide but there was nowhere. Before I knew what was happening, someone had grabbed me and was holding me tight his nails digging into my flesh. Why did he have to hold me so tight? I wouldn't be going anywhere. There was no escape. *(Man grabs her then holds her then inspects her as if inspecting an animal looking her up and down. He then throws her to the ground and tries to rape her but she scratches his face. He strikes her across the face)* Please have mercy!

Man: The whore wants mercy. I'll show her mercy. *(kicks her)*

Woman: Someone help me Please help me.

(The man goes to beat her with a stick he picks up from the ground)

Woman: *(trying to protect herself - screams)* Matt!

Man: *(finding it funny throws down the stick)* He won't help you. Your lover won't help you. No one can help you now. Whore! He set you up. Do you hear? He set you up. Your lover set you up! *(she backs away from him)*

Pharisee: Tell us your name woman.

Man: *(raises his hand to her)* Answer when you are spoken to harlot!

Woman: What - what can I say?

Man: Why the truth, damn you!

Woman: *(to audience)* The truth about what? *(thinking)* Had I been set up? Matt had escaped. That's true. *(Dawning on her)* He had been allowed to escape. It was me they wanted. I was to be an example. A scapegoat. They wanted me to confess. To name the names of all the men I had been with. They wanted me to take the guilt, the punishment...to be the scapegoat...led like a lamb to the slaughter! There hadn't been any men in my life apart from Matt... and James.

Man: I'll make her talk. *(he advances on her, hits her across the face and forces her to the floor)* I'll give her some of her own medicine. Teach her a lesson she'll never forget. I'll show the whore what it's all about...*(He tries to rape her. She screams and struggles to get free)*

Pharisee: Enough!

(The man gets up and spits at her in contempt)

Pharisee: Remember why we are here. We don't want to take a corpse to Rabbi Jesus now do we?

Man: The Temple that's where He'll be - Rabbi Jesus. He must condemn her to death. Moses' Law commands it. *(To woman – taunting and enjoying it)* Great stones, great boulders will smash out your brains. You will grovel in pain and everyone will watch you die. Throwing rock upon rock, stone upon stone, curse upon curse upon you as you scream for mercy – *(laughs)* and there will be none. No one can save you now.

Pharisee: Take her to Rabbi Jesus.

(The man grabs hold of her and drags her on a circuit to Jesus inciting the crowds to shout for her to be killed. Ad lib. 'Kill the whore,' etc. Crowd picks up rocks to stone her with as she is thrown at Jesus' feet.)

Pharisee: Master this woman has been caught in the very act of adultery. Moses in the Law commands that such a woman should be stoned to death. But what do you say?

(Jesus stoops down and writes on the ground with a stick.)

Woman: I couldn't believe it. Rabbi Jesus seemed to ignore my accusers completely. Everyone waited with baited breath but I felt calm. He…Rabbi Jesus was in complete control and I knew somehow that He was on my side…that He understood. If only He had been there when James died, I would have had the strength to carry on. I certainly wouldn't have tried to seek comfort in Matt. He should be here instead of me. He had planned to commit adultery. Planned to trap me just as they were trying to trap Jesus now. Matt had used his charm and like a fool, I had succumbed. Well now, I was paying for it.

Pharisee: *(impatiently)* Rabbi, tell us your answer.

Man: *(shouting)* Kill the whore. *(He gets the crowd to join him in shouting for blood. Jesus silences them after a few moments)*

Jesus: Let he who is without sin cast the first stone.

(The Pharisees exit. The man picks up a stone and goes to throw it. Jesus looks at him. He drops the stone and exits.)

Jesus: Woman, where are your accusers? Has no one condemned you?

Woman: No one, Lord.

Jesus: Then neither do I condemn you. Go and sin no more.

(Exit woman, then exit Jesus.)

Sketch:

Daughter of Abraham

(adapted from the original by Rev John F. Ward)

Woman: Yes it's me! Here I am again, standing up as straight as a doorpost. It's a week, exactly a week since He laid His hands on me. Some people said that it would have worn off by now. 'It won't last,' they said, 'she's been bent double for eighteen years now. In a few days time, it will be back you mark my words.' But it's not. I'm not bent double. Most of you are used to seeing me like this *(walks along bent double)* locked in this cruel position and stared at whenever I leave my home. But *(she straightens up)* I'm not locked in it any more.

At first, I was wary of bending over in case I couldn't straighten up again! I thought it was tempting Providence. How silly. I'm free. I'm healed. Out of Satan's grip at last, out of it completely. He did it. Jesus, the prophet from Nazareth. He was teaching here in our synagogue last week. All He did was lay His hands on me and I was healed. I could hardly believe it!

The President of the synagogue went ice cold with fury when he saw it. When he saw me standing up straight. I burst into tears. How could he be like that? I nearly shouted 'I didn't come here to be healed. I didn't expect it to happen. Not after eighteen years!'

You know it's the truth because most of you saw it. You were there. You would think I had broken some sacred law daring to be healed on the Sabbath! That Jesus had broken the Sabbath, broken God's law by healing me, brought God's displeasure on our synagogue.

That's what our beloved President thinks and that's why I'm worried. He won't want to see me in here again unless I'm bent double! Maybe I ought to stay away. Pray at home with friends and neighbours just as I have been doing since I was first healed. At least they are pleased. They can't keep away. They are so excited. They just rush in and kiss me, and embrace me, and then we all burst into praise.

No, I have to be seen in the synagogue as I am now – free... transformed. Jesus gave me back my dignity. I am no longer a laughing stock taunted by children. God was working through Him, though Jesus. If God had been against it, then Jesus could not have done it, could He? So, if it was wrong, if it was against the Law of Moses, then God broke His own Sabbath. What am I saying? But that's right, isn't it? Don't be offended please. I didn't mean to be blasphemous.

'The Sabbath was made for man, not man for the Sabbath,' that's what Jesus said. But our President seems to think that the Law is more important than God. Jesus healing me forces him to choose between them! Between God and the Law. Unless of course he says that Jesus healed me by the power of Beelzebub. Surely, he wouldn't say that, would he?

(There is a sound of angry voices. The President grabs the woman and is apparently going to throw her out)

President: *(to audience)* Listen to me all of you. If this woman tries to get past my doorkeepers again I'll have her flogged, is that clear? I know some of you take her side. I know some of you follow Jesus of Nazareth, listening to His pernicious teaching. Well, let me tell you something about Him. He's no Rabbi. He's a carpenter's son. A fraud – and I'll never allow Him to speak in my synagogue again!

(to woman) As for you, only when you repent will you be allowed to return to this synagogue. Only when you are prepared to stand up in public and express a sincere regret for what happened last week – will I be prepared to reconsider your position. *(pause)* But perhaps you will be willing to do so now. If so speak to these people here. *(pause)* Go on. *(pause)* Stop staring at me woman. *(pause)* Well?

Woman: *(defiantly)* He healed me.

President: A mere trifle compared to God's holy Law!

Woman: He healed me. Don't you understand? I'm free!

President: Nonsense. I'll hear no more of this. You should be ashamed...

Woman: I'm free! It is you who are chained. Shackled by the Law, and all those like you. Jesus is right. The Sabbath is made for man, not man for the Sabbath!

President: Silence!

Woman: He opened my eyes to the Truth. He proclaims liberty to the captives, freedom to those in prison.

President: Do not listen to this woman. I tell you...

Woman: He is a blind guide, a whited sepulchre.

President: Silence, I say! *(Ad lib throughout the next speech calling guards to throw her out by the end of the speech they have hold of her)*

Woman: Is there a single one of you, Jesus said, who does not loose his ox and his ass from it's stall and take it out to water on the Sabbath, but you won't let me do good to this woman. Here is a daughter of Abraham who has been bound by Satan for eighteen long years. Was it not right for her to be loosed from her bonds on the Sabbath day?

President: *(to woman in a fury)* You – you were healed by the power of Beelzebub, do you hear! Take her away.

Woman: *(whispers)* Father forgive.

Chapter 12

Yet More Healing

I have suffered from very bad hay fever since the age of nine, making every summer a misery. By summer, I mean May to September! One year however after prayer and ministry I had a whole summer where I had no trace whatsoever of the dreaded hay fever. I could picnic in parks, wander through cornfields, buy bunches of flowers, and enjoy being out in the garden. What bliss! This particular year, and this made it even more special to me, was an extremely bad year, a year when people who never usually suffered from hay fever were having a bad time of it, and here was I, totally free. I naturally expected never to have to suffer hay fever again, but the next year it was back and has been every year since. I have never been able to understand or explain it apart from 'the Lord gives, and the Lord takes away. Blessed be the name of the Lord.' Some said I must have sinned. Who hasn't? But nothing out of the ordinary, only 'venial' sins came to mind – (i.e. small, petty ones). You can tell I was brought up Roman Catholic. Some said I needed more ministry. Maybe? Whatever the reason, I am grateful that medication now keeps it under control so that summers aren't too bad. It would still be wonderful to be totally free from it once more and this possibility has never been ruled out.

When my son Philip was about seven years old I was due to do a solo performance of an Easter play booked at a local hall, and there I was laid on the sofa with no energy, hardly able to move, and to make matters worse my voice had gone completely. Philip said, 'The devil wants to stop you, Mummy' – to which I thought, 'Philip's right.' As Philip had been the one sensible enough to come up with this, I asked him to lay hands on me and pray for me, which he did. I then got up and did the performance. On arriving at the hall, it had not been opened for us and we had a job to find the man with the keys. It really did seem as though someone didn't want the performance to go ahead. There were some teenage boys from a local youth club at the performance many of whom had not heard the gospel, and none of whom had ever seen live theatre. The youth leader thanked me for performing telling me that the boys would never forget the experience they had been given. Thank you Philip, and thank you Lord!

Another time I was due to do a solo performance at a church and once again, I had lost my voice. I decided to go ahead despite advice from well meaning Christian friends to cancel. The performance included several songs for me to sing. The minute I stood up my voice came back and when the play finished, the voice disappeared and I had to speak to people in a whisper from then on. That will teach me to pray that I get my voice back 'just for the performance!' I do of course believe in 'Doctor Theatre', but even more so in prayer. The two together work extremely well in my experience.

I was diagnosed with keratoconnus about ten years ago. This is a condition where the cornea goes pointed so it's as if you are looking through bubble glass. As you can imagine it means you can't see very clearly. The doctors offered me a corneal graft which is a little like a transplant. My damaged cornea was replaced by a donor's cornea. The result of which is that I can see well enough to drive a car, which has made a tremendous difference to my life. To me this was a definite healing for which I am extremely grateful. Being a coward, I would have preferred the 'laying on of hands' followed by an immediate miracle, but this was not to be. My 'miracle' came at the hands of the surgeon. I still have to wear contact lenses permanently in order to get the correct vision, but that is a small price to pay, and who knows, my sight could yet be miraculously healed along with the eye that has not yet been operated on. Prior to the operation, I went up for the healing of my eyes time and time again in various meetings, often taking out my lenses to test whether I could see. I found these times very upsetting and frustrating. I do have a friend whose eyesight was miraculously healed. He used to wear glasses that looked like the bottom of a milk bottle for thickness, and was having no end of trouble with his eyesight. Now he can see perfectly without any glasses to do the intricate computer work connected with his music.

Healing is something that I will never understand. I have had many more healings over the years than I have shared, but still have to go to the doctor for some of my illnesses. Sat in a worship meeting a few weeks ago, I felt further healing taking place in my feet. My ankles still need strengthening and I hope that will happen soon. If I receive much more healing, I will have to 'act' when doing my Mary Magdalene sketch, and that will never do! When I first started to perform this sketch, I couldn't walk more that two or three steps in 'those shoes'. Now I can walk the length of a church. Soon I will have to pretend that I have a disability – praise the Lord!

*As Sarah in 'Mud and Stars'
a play set in a hospice, in which Sarah comes to
terms with life and death*

(photo: John Drury)

Sketch:

Esther

It was one whole year I had to wait, to prepare myself, to make myself ready, and then at last the day came. 'It maybe that you were born into the Kingdom for such a time as this,' my 'Uncle' Mordecai said, and looking back now, I'm sure that it was true that, Adonia our Almighty, Omnipotent, Omnipresent God had planned this from the beginning of time. Yet who would have thought it that I, Esther, the orphaned one, the one of no consequence, a girl, too, would have been chosen to bring about the salvation of my people, a people I hardly dared admit belonging to.

Everything in my life up to this point had been a preparation, a training ground. Not one thing that had happened had been wasted. All had been redeemed. My background, my circumstances, my looks, my personality. All had worked together for good, for our good, for the good of God's chosen people. Like my ancestor Joseph, it was God and not man who had placed me where I was. Joseph told his brothers not to be grieved or angry with themselves for selling him into slavery, for it was God who had sent him before to bring about the salvation of many, and now He was doing the same with me. And to think, the times I blamed God for letting me be born a girl, for allowing me to become orphaned, for causing me to have to live at Mordecai's house where there were so many tedious tasks to perform, everything needing to be done correctly and to the minutest detail. Having to cook and clean and scrub and scour, and nothing ever changed no matter how much I prayed or fasted, or recited the Torah!

I wanted to be in the Temple, listening to stories of my ancestors, not imprisoned in the home at Mordecai's beck and call. I wanted to do something important with my life, to be somebody, to do something only I could do, something that would be remembered forever. I wanted to be like my ancestor David. I would fight Goliath, I just needed the opportunity, that's all. Mordecai always said that I was a dreamer, but dreams can come true. Take Purim, for example, a time when my story is told in synagogues throughout the world to the clapping of hands, the stamping of feet, with bounteous blessings bestowed upon Mordecai and I, and clamorous curses shouted at Haman and the Jews enemies.

King Ahasuerus of Persia held a feast for all his nobles and Princes. On the seventh day of the feast when he was very drunk, he sent for Queen Vashti to come and show off her beauty to his guests. She refused. The King was furious and issued a decree under the law of the Medes and Persians that could not be revoked, to divorce her. Later, he regretted his actions. His advisors suggested that he find a replacement for Queen Vashti. The country was scoured, and I, Esther was one of the chosen – it was all part of God's plan of salvation, you see. Mordecai warned me to keep my ancestry a secret, so no one knew that I was a Jew, or that Mordecai was my relative.

Haman became the King's right hand man and everyone in the Kingdom had to bow down and worship him, and everyone did; that is, everyone apart from Mordecai who said that he would worship only Jehovah, the God of Israel. Haman was furious and knowing Mordecai to be a Jew, decided to rid the Kingdom of all Jews once and for all. So, like so many before him, and so many yet to come, he plotted against God's chosen, tricking the King into signing an edict under the law of the Medes and Persians. 'There is a certain people, your Majesty, scattered abroad and dispersed among the people in all the provinces of your Kingdom. Their laws are different from every other people; neither do they keep the King's laws. Therefore, it is not for the King's profit to tolerate them. If it pleases the King, let it be decreed that they be destroyed, and I will pay ten thousand talents of silver into the hands of those who have charge of the King's businesses that it may be brought into the King's treasuries.' Haman then cast lots or 'Pur' to decide the day of our destruction and the day was set for the thirteenth day of Adar.

When Mordecai heard of this, he came to me for help, asking me to go before the King to plead for my people. By this time, I had become the Queen of Persia. He said that I need not think that just because I was here in the Palace, I would be safe and escape their fate. He said that if I remained silent at such a time, then Jehovah would raise up help from elsewhere to save his people, but that I and my father's house would perish. I didn't know what to do. Maybe Mordecai was wrong, maybe no one would find out who I was. I was happy here in the Palace. I had everything I could ever want, and I was respected. It was all I had ever dreamed of, and besides, the King hadn't sent for me for thirty days. No one was allowed to go into his presence unless he sent for them. They did so at the risk of their lives. Only if the King held out the golden sceptre could they live, but I got no rest, no peace of mind until I decided not to stand by in silence and allow the extermination of my people. I fasted for three days along with my handmaiden, and Mordecai and all the Jews in Shushan prayed and fasted. At the end of three days, I knew what I must do. I went before the King and he held out the golden sceptre in my favour. He asked me what I desired, saying that I could have anything even up to half his Kingdom, but I asked only that he dine with me that night bringing Haman as our guest. At the banquet, the King again asked me what I desired and again I asked only that he dine with me the next day and bring Haman as our guest. Haman was delighted and no doubt boasted of this. Nothing could spoil his joy, nothing that is apart from Mordecai who still refused to bow the knee. On the advice of Zeresh, his wife, Haman had a gallows built sixty cubits high on which he purposed to hang Mordecai. That night, however, the King couldn't sleep and sent for the book of memorable deeds, the Chronicles to be read. Here he discovered that Mordecai had uncovered a plot against his life and had never been rewarded. When Haman arrived the next morning to ask permission to hang Mordecai, before he could speak the King asked him what should be done for a man whom the King delights to honour. Haman thinking that this man must surely be he himself, let his pride and imagination run away with him. 'Let him be dressed in the royal robes of blue and white with the royal crown upon his head. Let him ride upon the King's horse and be led through the streets of the city of Shushan by one of the King's noblest Princes declaring, 'this is the man the King delights to honour'.' The King then told Haman to do this for Mordecai the Jew, and that is how Haman came to be leading Mordecai through the streets of Shushan declaring, 'This is the man the King delights to honour.' When his wife heard of this, she predicted that if Mordecai against whom he was fighting was a Jew, he would not prevail against him but would fall before him. With this prediction ringing in his ears, Haman was escorted to my banquet. The King once more asked me what I desired. The time had now come to speak. I told him of the plight of my people, and of Haman's deception. Letters were sent throughout the Kingdom allowing the Jews to arm themselves on the day set for our destruction, and many became Jews that day, for the fear of the Jews fell upon them. Haman was hanged on his own gallows, and Mordecai, who the King now knew to be my relative, was honoured and given all Haman's wealth and the signet ring belonging to the King. On the day set for our destruction, the Jews were victorious against their enemies.

Throughout history, there has always been a Haman. There has always been an Esther – those willing to risk their lives for the salvation of their people. Those remaining faithful and prayerful. Those who come alongside their Jewish brothers and become their friends. Those who become their enemies. To each is given a choice; to love or to hate. To do good, or to do evil. Whoever you are, whatever you are, like me, you must choose, for no one knows what the future will hold or when the voice will say, 'It maybe that you were born into the Kingdom for such a time as this.'

Chapter 13

Mother-in-Law

What a difficult chapter to write. The very term 'mother-in-law' sends a shiver down many a spine! Had I been writing this three weeks ago, I would have played with words and very appropriately called it 'mother-in-law's tongue', my husband being a gardener. However, three weeks ago, this chapter would not have been written at all, as it is only in the last two weeks that things have happened that I would like to share. Ten days ago my mother-in-law died and this chapter is a tribute to her and a testimony to God's healing of relationships. God's tremendous love was shown to us in so many ways at this time and I hope that this story will help heal many hurting relationships.

In common with many daughters-in-law, I could do no right. I was not a good housewife, a good mother or the 'right' person to be married to Andrew. I didn't dress correctly, have the right hairstyle or choose the right house or area to live in, to name but a few. In fact, the only thing I did do right was to provide the three grandchildren. Throughout the years, everything I did or said was criticised and after twenty or so years, I had had enough. From then onwards, I visited only very spasmodically. Then, my mother-in-law had a stroke about three years ago. We travelled from Birmingham to York to visit her in hospital and made sure, that we, that is my husband and I, kept in touch by telephone and by visiting as often as possible. During her time in hospital, we bought her a Christian book and shared the Gospel with her. She was very appreciative and her personality seemed to change dramatically. It became a real pleasure to visit her and to talk to her. The critical nature disappeared to a large extent and was replaced by kindness and understanding. It is so sad that it took an illness to cause this change of heart. I often think of all the wasted years and what could have been.

As a result of the stroke, my mother-in-law found movement difficult and was forced to be very dependent on her husband. Being a very determined person, she was adamant that she should have a motorised scooter in place of the old wheelchair in order to become a little more independent. This meant selling the Suzuki Baleno and buying a 'people carrier' which had a boot capable of transporting the scooter. She was also determined that we should buy their 'old' car at an extremely reasonable price. We bought it on Saturday, and by midnight on Tuesday, she had died. I telephoned her on the Monday night to reassure her that I had managed to drive the car successfully through the centre of Birmingham at rush hour. It was a very big car and I had been worried about driving it. She said that she was very pleased that I had managed and that she hoped that we would have many happy hours with the car. It is only four years old and totally unlike our old car which we used to drive. My mother-in-law was also instrumental in us selling our old car to the daughter of a friend who lived in York who had just passed her driving test. We drove to York in our old car, sold it there and returned to Birmingham in our brand new car. My mother-in-law was delighted to have been of help.

I had bought a coat and a suit in the sales in York and I showed them to my mother-in-law. She commented that I couldn't have made a better choice. What a change from the criticism I was used to from her. The colour, the style – everything, she said – was perfect. The last Saturday we saw her alive, she made us a really special meal which I now call our Last Supper. At the time, I remember saying, 'Lord, why is this happening?' I assumed that it was because we hadn't been able to spend Christmas with her, but now of course I know the real reason. The next day with my help, she cooked us a Sunday dinner. We usually went out for this, but she was determined to cook for us. It was the final meal we had with her. Before I left, she told me what a help I had been to her and said we were welcome to come and stay any time. Again, a real change to the comments I had become used to over the years, and all the more precious as physically having guests was not at all easy for her. We left York after Sunday lunch, and by Tuesday midnight, Mum had died...

We were given the sad news of her death by a friend with a spare key coming into our bedroom at 1.30 am. Our downstairs phone had been ringing, but we had been so tired that we hadn't heard it. Apparently, my father-in-law had phoned my daughter Lindy who also being unable to contact us had phoned our neighbour David to get the message to us. We set off to York the following morning in order to help and to comfort my father-in-law. I was able to clear 'Mum's' clothes and personal effects for him. We sent the clothes to the Russian Jews, which helped us to give them away more easily, as we knew that they were going to a good cause, and one close to our heart. I also arranged the chapel service. Andrew's Mum had started to attend the local Methodist chapel on occasional Sundays, and the Friendship Hour regularly after having her stroke. Then I arranged the crematorium service and the final family get-together that was to follow the funeral. I had recently been to a family funeral in York where the wake had been held in a hotel. It was dreadful. The room was too small and chairs had not been arranged correctly, which meant that the mourners were not able to reminisce together and support each other in a way that would have been helpful, and the food was not very good. I decided that we would not have this as I wanted the 'do' at Mum's funeral to be as relaxed and happy as possible, a place where people could remember, and encourage one another, while sharing in their grief. I booked a pub with a carvery. My friends would not be surprised about this! How this came about is another story. On our arrival in York, we went to the morgue to view the body. When we arrived at reception, a voice from twenty years ago greeted me. My friend Carol had been working at the hospital for the past eleven years. I told her my misgivings about holding the 'do' at the hotel, and a lady working alongside her suggested the venue that we chose of which she had heard many good reports, and we were not disappointed. People clustered together happily talking. It was all that I could have hoped for. It was a healing time for those gathered, and Mum would have been well pleased. A relative commented, 'Why does it take this to get a family together?' Why does it?

For me it was a real privilege to do all the arranging and everything that happened became part of a healing process in my life. The chapel service itself was a real blessing. My main thought was, 'What would Mum have wanted?' For her birthday the previous July, we, that is my husband, my daughter Anna and her boyfriend Tim, my son Philip and his fiancée, Jenny, my eldest daughter Lindy and her two sons, Matthew aged three, and Cameron aged two, and I (the instigator), went to visit her. Anna, Tim and Andrew had made a CD for mum, which consisted of many of the old hymns. My husband sang some of these as solos, with my daughter Anna or Tim playing the accompaniment. One or two of the songs were duets, with my daughter Anna and my husband singing together. One of the songs my daughter Anna and I had written together, and one was a song of mine that Anna had improved upon. Mum was delighted with the whole thing. It was great to play that trick on her, all with the best of motives. I remember telephoning her saying, 'I hope your birthday card arrives on time. I've been so busy that I've only just posted it. I'll send your present later' – knowing full well that the whole contingent of us, complete with birthday tea, CD, and presents were about to descend on her as a birthday surprise. Andrew's Dad was in on the act. He played his part admirably. It really was a surprise to Mum when we arrived. The CD became, in her own words, her 'Sunday Service'. When she first listened to it, she wept. There was her son singing the old familiar hymns. Matthew, my, I should say, 'our' three-year-old grandson was there in the bedroom listening to the CD with her. When it came to 'Steal Away' he said to me, 'Granny, that's really sad' and started to sob. 'No, Matthew,' I said, 'it's not sad. It's about how Jesus will help us when we need Him'. Then I thought, 'Yes, Matthew, you're right, Negro spirituals are sad'. Out of the mouths of babes! We continued playing the CD. 'Grandma' sobbing, overwhelmed by what we had done, and no doubt by the words, reminding her of her childhood chapel days when she had had a simple faith in a God of love. Little Matthew was also sobbing, unaware of 'Grandma's' plight, so much so that I had to take him from the room. Can God really touch a child's heart in such a way? I know He can.

Back to the funeral, what a blessing. I read two poems that Mum had written out. I had asked Dad for some paper on which to write out ideas for the funeral service. He handed me an exercise book. There on the first page was a poem about smiling. I would print it here, but maybe it has copyright. A day or so later, he produced yet another poem that mum had copied out, this time about resting at night in order to gain strength and be equipped to do God's will in the morning. To me, they showed two sides of the same person, Mum. The chapel funeral service fitted together perfectly. Dad chose a piece of harp music for the beginning of the service, after which I read John 3 v 14 – 18A:

> "Just as Moses lifted up the snake in the desert, so the Son of Man *must* be lifted up, that everyone who believes in him may have eternal life.
>
> "For God so loved the world that he gave his one and only Son, that whoever believes in him shall not perish but have eternal life. For God did not send his Son into the world to condemn the world, but to save the world through him. Whoever believes in him is not condemned..."

followed by I Corinthians Chapter 15 v *55:*

> "Where, O death, is your victory?
> Where, O death, is your sting?"

and John 14 v 1-3:

> "Do not let your hearts be troubled. Trust in God; trust also in me. In my Father's house are many rooms; if it were not so, I would have told you. I am going there to prepare a place for you. And if I go and prepare a place for you, I will come back and take you to be with me that you also may be where I am."

Anna then sang a song that she and Tim had written and composed especially for the occasion. Tim accompanied the hymns and Anna's solo on the piano, Anna joining him on the trumpet for the final hymn 'Great is Thy Faithfulness'. Andrew said a few words and prayed. He also had arranged the flowers that were on the coffin, which was led out to his solo of 'Amazing Grace' from Mum's famous birthday CD. Another of his solos, 'Turn Your Eyes Upon Jesus,' was played both as we entered and left the crematorium. It was truly a family affair of which Mum would have been proud, orchestrated by the loving Unseen Hand of Father God...

Song:

The Pictures Will Remain In Our Heart

written and composed by Timothy Davies and Anna Appleyard

Verse 1:

> Your smile sends the storms away
> and the flowers start to grow
> To be picked, to be loved
> that's the way we'll always know

Verse 2:

> And their colours they will shine
> above our souls to be protected
> The sound they make, the words they speak
> that's the way we'll always know

Bridge:

> When the wind turns
> you'll turn it back again
> with every tear we shed
> the flower glows

Chorus:

> The pictures will remain in our heart
> The pictures will remain in our heart
> Every season of the year
> You'll be watching us,

Any time of the day
You'll be watching us,
The pictures will remain in our heart
The pictures will remain in our heart.

Repeat VERSE 1 & 2

The Pictures will remain in our heart

In memory of Cley Appleyard

Words and Music by
A. Appleyard & T. Davies

© 2001 copyright by A. Appleyard & T. Davies

Chapter 14

Barriers

In a prayer meeting at our church recently, three men, big men, about six foot and weighty, were told to stand in the aisle blocking it completely. Jean, a friend of mine, like me less than five feet tall, was then told to push through the men. 'You may feel that they are a huge barrier' she was told,' but when you step out in faith you will discover that it is not as difficult as you thought it would be because they will not fight against you'. A picture of a truth, I know, but as she physically obeyed and pushed through there was no real resistance. How true - that which we fear is often nothing but shadows and sham. A pastor then commented that this was only a picture. Knowing Jean, she like me, had watched many men literally creating barriers in her life, all her life, and these 'barriers' were real. She is at present writing her own autobiography 'My Life, my Crime, my God'. Jean had murdered her boyfriend after years of abuse from him, and from all other men in her life. She became a Christian soon after, and only served six months of her sentence. I knew that God was showing us both that in reality we had to press forward, and not fear the face of man, in our case literally 'man'.

In my life, I think I was my own worst 'barrier'. In my thought life, I was so negative. Hence my prayer, 'Lord, please don't let me stand in the way of the blessings that You wish to bestow on me!' You name it; I think I can't do it. Thank the Lord for friends who speak out against this. I have only ever painted one oil painting entitled 'Changes' (on the front cover). A friend recently looked at it and said 'why ever did you stop?' The picture framer said 'If it is your one and only then it deserves to be framed.' A change of attitude is all it takes to break down the barriers.

People often tend to look on the outward appearance; I do, too. That's why some of my sketches home in on this. How wrong we often tend to be.

I met one lady 'missionary' in appearance, very precise and capable, and immediately thought that she would look down on me, 'a chaotic being'. When in York one day shopping, I prayed that the Lord would send me someone I could really talk to, as I desperately needed this. Who should round the corner a few seconds later, but this lady? We had an honest chat, and became the best of friends.

A vicar at a church I once attended looked at what he thought he saw, and judged, or should I say mis-judged, like so many others have done. He was present at a house group meeting on one particular occasion when I shared honestly a little about my life. In front of all the group this vicar apologised, saying, 'I'm sorry, I didn't know. I didn't understand. I now know that I put many barriers in your way. Please forgive me.' It was wonderful to be vindicated like this, but that vicar was just leaving the parish at this point, and when a new one took over the 'barriers' were erected once more. No wonder that we are told that we are in a battle.

'For we wrestle not against flesh and blood, but against principalities, against powers, against the rulers of the darkness of this world, against spiritual wickedness in high places'.

Ephesians 6 v 12.

I do, however, always hope for better, especially from my Christian brothers and sisters.

Poem:

Flame

Written by Linda Mae

Flame dancing in the breeze

Swaying

reaching Heavenwards

straining

upwards…upwards…upwards

dancing

reaching

burning

With desire to touch

YOU

GOD JEHOVAH

MESSIAH

LORD

Poem:

Rose Petal Tears

written by Linda Mae

Rose petal tears
dropping
Mourning for the lost
JEWS.
In Remembrance
Of those, fated – destroyed
By those who knew not what they do.

Rose petal tears
dropping
Mourning for the lost
ABORTED ONES.
In Remembrance
Of those, deprived of life –
God – given
By those who know not what they do.

Rose petal tears
dropping
Mourning for the lost
SOULS
In remembrance
Of those, eternal life denying – dying
For they know not what they do.

FATHER FORGIVE

Chapter 15

Jews

I do not understand this, but by the age of eight, I was praying 'Lord, it's not fair, why couldn't I have been born one of your chosen people?' Somehow, without actually saying it, the Roman Catholic nuns who had taught me had made me aware that the Jews are extra special to God, and are 'God's chosen people.' I know Topol in 'Fiddler on the Roof' cries, 'Lord, couldn't you have chosen someone else?' But what a privilege!

From as far back as I can remember I have had a love for the Jews. It has to be God given, and is no doubt for a purpose, because otherwise it just doesn't make sense.

When my husband and I sold our semi-detached house in York so we could move to Birmingham for me to attend Drama School, we saved money from the sale to visit Israel for our holiday of a lifetime. Since then, we have been back five times. When they ask at Customs why we are coming back yet again, we say that it's because it is the most wonderful place in the world! And to us, it is.

On our first visit to Israel, we went to Yad Vashem. I couldn't speak for hours afterwards. I felt so guilty at belonging to a race that could do such a thing. The room dedicated to the children made an enormous impression on me. The dark, the candles, the mirrors, the photos on screen, the names of each child being read, with their country of origin and age, was so moving. I stole the idea to a degree; using it in a play I was producing which deals with the subject of abortion. At the beginning of my play, a slide of a foetus was projected on to a screen. Then images of children playing appeared on the screen, with a recording of children singing nursery rhymes and enjoying themselves in the playground. Innocence. Innocence in the instance of abortion, cut short by a mother's choice, in the instance of the holocaust, by hatred, prejudice and anti-Semitism.

Even in the church still, I believe there is often anti-Semitism. I find it hard to understand why when we, as Christians, are followers of 'Jesus of Nazareth, King of the Jews', and when our Messiah is Yeshua, born in Bethlehem, and crucified in Jerusalem. A song I once started to write says, 'Jesus was a Jew. How about you? Gentile grafted into the tree – the wild olive tree.'

If we have truly been grafted in then maybe that makes us Jewish, too?

Sketch:

Hadassah

Enter Habal dragging Esther by a rope. Her hands are bound.

Habal: Come on. Hurry up. You too slow. You Jews!

Habal unbinds her and throws her to the ground.

Habal: Welcome to your new home. You Jewish bitch!

Esther: *(as if reciting a prayer)* The Lord is my rock, my fortress and my deliverer *(repeats this)*

Habal: You want some of me, huh?

As Habal is about to attack her, she scratches his face.

Esther: No!

Habal retaliates by striking Esther.

Habal: You Jewish bitch! I tie you good. You do not deserve freedom.

Habal ties Esther's hands behind her back and exits. There is some water in a dish. Esther crawls towards it and tries to lap up the water.

Esther: *(as a prayer)* Help me. Help me. Lord Jehovah, please help me. Help me. Help me please help me!

Habal: Quiet. You be quiet.

Esther: Help me. Help me. Please help me.

Habal: Shut up.

Esther: Help me. Help me.

Habal: *(as he enters)* Too loud. Too much talk.

Habal kicks Esther.

Esther: *(quietly)* Help me. Please help me.

Habal: How I help you?

Esther: I'm hungry.

Habal: *(loosening his sash)* Is good? You want more of me?

Esther: *(with contempt)* Food. I want food. Food I want food.

Habal: Food? You want food. I got food.

Habal spits at her and goes towards the food...

Habal: No you not have this. This too good for you. I eat...

Habal sits and eats an apple.

Esther: *(as a prayer)* The Lord is my rock, my fortress and my deliverer *(repeats this)*

Habal re-enters carrying a pan of soup and some bread. He feeds the bread to Esther as if feeding an animal.

Habal: Good, huh? You like bread. I give you bread.

Habal becomes bored dropping the bread on the floor. He watches in amusement as Esther tries to eat it.

Esther: Cut me loose.

Habal holds the pan of soup to her lips.

Habal: Take.

Esther: Cut me loose. My arms are hurting.

Habal: Too much like this huh *(he mimes her scratching him)*

Esther: I won't, I promise.

Habal: No good this, huh? No good!

Esther: I won't scratch.

Habal: Take.

Esther: I promise I won't scratch.

Habal pulls her head back to make her eat

Habal: Take!

Esther: I won't scratch I promise.

Habal: Take!

Esther takes a gulp of soup then realises what it is and spits it in Habal's face.

Habal: Bitch! You Jewish bitch. I teach you!

Habal picks up the whip, raises it and goes towards Esther

Esther: *(vehemently)* It's pork. You've given me pork. It's pork. You've given me pork!

Habal: Pork? Ah – pig... Oink...oink...*(he laughs throwing down the whip)* Oink, oink. My little Jewish princess. She not like pork. It is so funny. The Jews they do not like pork. *(exits kicking the water over as he goes)*

Esther: The Lord is my rock, my fortress and my deliverer. *(repeats this and eventually falls asleep)*

Habal enters carrying some water, a cloth and a bag. He kicks Esther

Habal: Oink, oink, oink, oink, *(slaps her face to wake her up)*. Hey no asleep, huh? No asleep.

Habal cuts Esther loose

Habal: I cut – but not like this, OK *(mimes scratching his face)* You good, huh?

Habal pulls Esther's limp body into a sitting position and begins to clean her face roughly with a cloth and put makeup on her.

Habal: We make you good, huh? We make you beautiful. Up, up!

Habal pulls Esther to her feet and throws a white dress at her.

Habal: So. Put on.

Esther: Why?

Habal: Put.

Esther: What for?

Habal: Business. Nothing to do with you.

Esther: Turn your back.

Habal: Quickly, quickly!

Esther: Turn your back.

Habal: Is no time! No time!

Esther: Turn your back.

Habal: Why you think so big, huh? You think I want for me? *(mimes scratching face)* Pah, you stink!

Esther stands until Habal turns away and then takes off her dress. As she is doing this, Habal turns round.

Habal: *(aside)* Not bad for a Jewish girl.

Esther notices him watching

Esther: *(challenging him)* Turn your back!

Habal: *(cracking the whip)* Put on now or I give you such a beating!

Esther puts on the dress. Habal takes her to the edge of the stage Esther resisting the whole time.

Habal: *(to audience)* Anyone want to buy a good Jewish slave? Very strong. *(to Esther)* Show your teeth *(tries to make her)* Show them your teeth. Anyone want to buy? Very cheap.

Enter Mordecai. Habal guides Esther in his direction

Habal: Good girl, huh? Very healthy. Very strong.

Mordecai: *(noticing the scratch on Habal's face)* So I see.

Habal: Yes well...*(caressing Esther's hair)* Beautiful, huh? Finest quality.

Mordecai: What's her name?

Habal: *(shrugs curiously and tries to remember)* Esther.

Esther: Sir, you're wasting your money.

Mordecai: *(to Esther)* I mean your real name, not the one they gave you.

Esther: I promise you sir, you are wasting your money.

Mordecai: At meribet hivrit.

Esther: You're a Hebrew?

Mordecai: What tribe?

Esther: Benjamin.

Mordecai: How long have you been here? I promise it will not count against you.

Esther: I don't know...about forty days.

Mordecai: And before that?

Esther: We lived in Jerusalem. One night a raiding party came from Aram...The soldiers chose four of us to...

Mordecai: And the others – your family?

Esther: I don't know.

Mordecai: You do have a family?

Esther: Abihail...They were called Abihail.

Mordecai: Were? You mean? You don't have to say any more. How often does he feed you? Again, I promise it will not count against you.

Esther: He gives me bread.

Mordecai: And pig meat? Which you've eaten*? (Esther nods)* It's all right. Don't worry.

Habal: She is good for you, huh? Strong.

Mordecai tosses a bag of coins to Habal who is overjoyed until he sees the amount

Mordecai: Oh you are quite right Habal. A woman like this should fetch twenty, twenty-five, even thirty. So, you would be wise in the future to take care of your investment. Even a monster like you should see the economic sense that makes. Now leave us.

Habal: You Jews. You're all the same *(Habal spits at Esther)*

Habal: *(to Mordecai)* You stink. You Jews you all stink! *(exits)*

Mordecai beckons to Esther

Esther: I don't care who you are. I will not be bought.

Mordecai: Oh, Hadassah. Don't you know me? Don't you know who I am? I'm Mordecai. I'm your relative, Mordecai.

As Esther in a scene from 'Hadassah'
Performed at the Christian Artists' Seminar, Doorn, Holland,
in 1999, with Nick Breakspear Jones as Habal, a slave trader.

Photo: Dimitri Tsouris

*Nick Breakspear Jones as Habal
a slave trader in 'Hadassah'*

photo: Dimitri Tsouris

Sketch:

Purim

(A production of this type is performed in synagogues throughout the world on the thirteenth and fourteenth day of Adar (March) to celebrate the Jewish feast of Purim, which was instituted by Queen Esther to celebrate the Jews' victory over their enemies)

(The King is seated on his throne goblet in hand. There is an empty throne beside him Haman is standing downstage left. Upstage right are Queen Vashti and her ladies having their own party. The narrator is downstage right)

Narrator: *(downstage right)* This is the story of the great and powerful Ahasuerus.

All: Who saw us? *(a placard is held up. Haman encourages everyone to join in)*

Narrator: Aha - saw - us.

All: Oh, Ahasuerus!

Narrator: Ahasuerus ruled over one hundred and twenty seven provinces stretching from India to Cush. Such a powerful monarch demanded instant obedience. One day he decided to hold a feast, a party for all his nobles and officials. On the seventh day of the feast when he was very drunk, he demanded that Queen Vashti who was

	having a banquet with all the ladies should come and show off her beauty to his guests.
King:	*(clicks his fingers and then beckons to Haman)* Go and tell the Queen that she must come here now.
Haman:	*(goes over to Vashti)* The King wants you to come show off your beauty to his guests.
Queen Vashti:	*(stamping her foot)* No I don't want to. I won't come!
Haman:	*(Going over to the King)* The Queen refuses to come your majesty. *(Haman bows and then returns to downstage left)*
King:	*(angrily)* She won't come. What do you mean she won't come! What if all the other women in the Kingdom follow her example? I must do something. What am I going to do?
Narrator:	Such a King never lacked advisors, in this case Memucan.
All:	*(Haman holds up cue card)* Who can?
Narrator:	Memu - can.
All:	Oh, Memu - can!
Narrator:	Memucan
All:	Oh, Memucan - can!
Memucan:	Why not divorce her your Majesty and find a new Queen to take her place?
King:	It shall be done. We will have a beauty contest to which all the most beautiful women in the

country will come and I will choose myself a new Queen, *(he clicks his fingers and Haman takes the crown off Queen Vashti and gives it to the King. Then all the ladies including Esther parade round in a circle for the beauty contest. They enter from the audience)*

Narrator: So a beauty contest was held at the Palace and one of the people there was Esther the adopted daughter of Mordecai the Jew and it was she who was chosen to be Queen.

King: *(Pointing at Esther)* I'll have that one. I like her. *(He puts the crown upon her head. Esther then stays beside the king throughout sitting on her throne)*

Narrator: And so it was that Esther, the adopted daughter of Mordecai the Jew was chosen to be queen. Now when Haman became the King's right hand man, he became prouder and prouder. He asked the king to issue a decree that everyone throughout the kingdom should bow down and worship him, and everyone did, everyone that is but Mordecai.

(People come up from the audience and walk past Haman and as they do, all stop and bow down to him. Then enter Mordecai complete with prayer shawl. He walks up and down praying, sees Haman and does not bow down to him)

Haman: That Jew Mordecai refuses to bow down and worship me. Me, Haman the great. He must pay for this insult. I will ask the king if I can destroy Mordecai and all of the Jews. That will teach him to disobey me!

Narrator:	So Haman tricked the king into issuing a decree that said all the Jews throughout the kingdom must be killed. When Mordecai heard about this, he sent a message to Esther asking her to go before the king and plead for her people. Esther did not know what to do because no one could just go before the king, and the king has not sent for her for forty days, and unless he held out the golden sceptre in her favour allowing her to remain, she would be put to death. But Mordecai told her not to think that just because she was living in the palace she would escape the fate of her people. 'It may be that you have been brought to the kingdom for just such a time as this,' he said. Esther decided to pray for three days along with her servants and handmaiden, and the Jewish people also fasted and prayed.
Esther	*(Standing up and walking to downstage centre)* I will go to the king and if I die, I die.
Narrator:	After three days, Esther went in to the king and he held out the golden sceptre out in her favour. He said that she could have anything she wanted even up to half his kingdom.

(Esther turns and goes to the king and bows at his feet. He holds out the golden sceptre. She then gets up and stands before him)

King:	Queen Esther you can have anything you want even up to half my kingdom. *(She sits back on the throne)*

Narrator:	Esther asked that the king attend a banquet that she had prepared and that he bring Haman along as their guest. At the banquet, the king again asked Esther what she desired even up to half his kingdom and again Esther asked the king to a banquet the following day with Haman as their guest. Haman was very proud of this honour but when Mordecai again refused to bow down before him, he was furious. Mordecai believed that he should only bow down to worship the God of Israel. Haman had a gallows built on which to hang Mordecai. The king could not sleep that night and sent for the book of memorable deeds to be brought to him.
King:	*(clapping his hands)* Bring me the book of memorable deeds. *(a servant brings it to him)*
Narrator:	There he read how Mordecai uncovered a plot against his life and found that Mordecai had never been rewarded. Just then, Haman arrived to ask if he could hang Mordecai but before he could speak the king asked him.
King:	What should be done to a man who I, the king, wish to honour?
Narrator:	Thinking that the King must mean he himself, Haman let his pride and imagination run away with him.
Haman:	Let him be dressed in royal robes, be given the King's crown to wear and one of the King's horses to ride and let him be led through the

	streets of the city by one of the King's noblest princes declaring 'this is the man the king delights to honour'.
King:	Go and do this for Mordecai the Jew.
Esther:	And that is how Haman came to be leading Mordecai through the city shouting 'This is the man the king delights to honour.'

(He leads Mordecai round on a hobby horse, the audience shouting and cheering 'Hooray. Three cheers for Mordecai.' The King holds up the cue card for this and encourages them)

Haman:	This is the man the man the king delights to honour. *(while he leads Mordecai around the audience)*
Esther:	*(stands)* At the banquet, I will tell the king the truth about my people. *(She sits)*
Narrator:	At last the time came again for the banquet and again the king asked what Esther desired.
King:	*(To Esther)* Tell me what you want, even up to half my kingdom and I will give it to you.
Esther:	Your majesty, I and my people will die unless you will help us.
King:	Who would dare to do such a thing?
Narrator:	Esther told the king that Haman had tricked him into signing an edict for the destruction of her people.
Esther:	Your majesty Haman has tricked you. Please, your Majesty, save my people. *(Esther falls on her knees before the king)*

King:	Take him away. *(Two soldiers lead Haman away)*
Narrator:	The King had Haman hanged on the gallows and Esther's people were saved from destruction.

(Audience members at Purim cheer and rattle football rattles when the name Esther or Mordecai are announced, and boo and hiss and stamp their feet when Haman is mentioned. Everyone has the letter 'H' written in chalk on the soles of their shoes, which is wiped off by the stamping by the end of the performance. Audience members can be Vashti, Esther, Mordecai, Memucan, beauty contest entrants (including some of the men), soldiers, a servant, Vashti's ladies-in-waiting and people bowing before Haman. Any words are put on cards complete with cue lines. The audience can also do the lines for 'ALL' with cue cards being held for them to see and encouragement from the King and Haman).

Song:

Beautiful Jerusalem

*words by Andrew Appleyard and Linda Mae
music by Anna Appleyard*

Verse 1:

    We see your beauty
    We see how fair you are Jerusalem
    For you are decked and fair
    As a bride adorned, prepared for her Husband.

Verse 2:

    We see your radiance
    You are fair to behold Jerusalem
    Like us - a Bride
    A Bride adorned, ready for her Husband.

Chorus:

    We behold your beauty
    We take of your wine
    For you are His
    And He is mine
    I take of your beauty
    And take of your wine
    Partakers in Messiah.

Verse 3:

    Some will try to steal
    For you are His, the Messiah Lord, and mine
    Some will try to spoil
    Jerusalem, city holy, set apart.

Verse 4:
> They see your beauty
> They see that you are fair Jerusalem
> They see the jewels
> Adorning you as you await your Lord.

Chorus:

Verse 5:
> He will rebuild us
> He will come with vengeance to defend
> Oh Jerusalem
> His Bride, His precious one, together we.

Verse 6:
> He will defend us both
> Messiah King, Yeshua, Jesus, Lord
> United as His Bride
> Both Jew and Gentile entwined and one

Chorus:

Verse 7:
> He will take us both
> For you are beautiful and so are we
> Oh Israel - His Bride
> Bride of Messiah King, King of Jerusalem.

Repeat VERSE 1

> As a beautiful Bride O beautiful Jerusalem.

Chapter 16

German

As someone born half German, I was both proud and ashamed at one and the same time. Germans have very good traits, being hardworking and single minded, and yet there is the legacy of anti-Semitism.

Having a German Dad, who proudly belonged to the Hitler Youth, who was a Nazi, and a German grandfather, a Communist, who had a mistress in the next village, and who beat his German wife and his children, I was not proud of my German blood. My aunty Elly was known in the village as 'the brave little Garbe' when she was going to school as a young child. This is one time I do not wish to read between the lines. What a childhood.

My father, so I believe, was beaten for any misdemeanour of his two sisters. He grew up with some typical German attitudes. Women were rubbish – child bearers and skivvies, not worthy of respect. They were there in his mind to be used, like doormats. Sons were to be cherished and respected, although he didn't actually manage it in practice as poor Michael my half-brother found to his cost.

Not surprisingly, I have, or had, a problem with German men. My eldest daughter at one time had a German boyfriend, and now my youngest daughter has one. Perhaps it's something to do with being a quarter German and finding your roots?

However, the Lord is now healing me. My daughter's boyfriend is a very nice young man, much better for knowing. First impressions showed him to be very German, and very abrupt in manner, which I found difficult to accept, given my background. In reality, though he has a good sense of humour and is very kind and helpful. I think the healing first started at Christian Artists' Seminar, Doorn, Holland, in 1998. There was a German artist there, Eckhard. I never actually spoke to him, I just watched. Here was a man who appeared very happy and laid back, and who had an obvious sense of humour – and he was German. I could hardly believe what I was seeing. In 1999, I actually spoke to him for a few seconds. What's difficult about that you may think? Well nothing, but for me it was a real milestone. Unfortunately, it is not just German men I had a problem with, but any man who remotely reminded me of my father in looks, age or manner. I had, and sometimes still have, difficulty in approaching them.

At the Christian Artists' Seminar in 2000, the healing still continued. I was disappointed to find that Eckhard had not attended this time, as I was now looking forward to chatting to him, and was considering involving him in one of the sketches that I was thinking of performing. Maybe next year? As it turned out, I needed someone to play Jesus on the cross for the sketch entitled 'Crucifixion'. Not an easy task, as the person concerned had to wear a loin cloth, and a crown of thorns and have a cross beam across his shoulders and stand on a plinth for about five or six minutes. I prayed for the right person to be available. Two people that I asked were honest enough, and brave enough, to say 'no'. I thanked them later, as I know how difficult it is to do this. If they had said 'yes', then I believe that the person of God's choice would have been denied the opportunity of taking part, and he was just perfect! When I turned, as Mary, and looked at Tourston, being Jesus on the cross, I could not believe it. No one could have looked the part more, and the effect on the audience and in people's lives was tremendous, so powerful. And guess what, Tourston, is a lovely German man with a great sense of humour, very laid back, happy, and gentle – a pleasure to work with. He got stage blood on his T-shirt from the rehearsal and said that he was not going to wash it off – it would be a souvenir of his performance.

In some drama workshops which I led, there were two young Germans, Walter and David. People who attended were expected to come to all eight sessions. These two came and asked permission to go along to one of the storytelling workshops. They were so respectful and polite, and I got the feeling that if I said 'No', they would have stayed for the drama workshop and not have gone to the storytelling one. Of course I said 'Yes, go and enjoy it and when you come back tell us all what you have learnt. ' Healing comes in so many ways, often in the simplest of actions.

When I visited my family in Germany several years ago, it helped a great deal. On arriving at the airport in Germany, I sobbed. I couldn't help it. It was as though I had come home. This was the second my feet touched German soil, before we had even reclaimed our baggage. I didn't know whether my relatives would recognise me, but they knew who I was immediately, and welcomed my husband and me.

It was here, in Germany, that I found the completion of my roots, both in Berlin, and in Waltersdorf where my Dad had been born. I fitted in so well, that someone in the village where my aunt lived thought that I was her daughter; there was such a family resemblance. I had only met this branch of my family once, when I was nine, and when they lived behind the Iron Curtain. This time, I felt so 'at home' with them that I relaxed and sat on a chair how I wanted to sit, with my right leg tucked under so that I sat on it. This was a family trait which I knew nothing about. They were delighted at this, the interpreter, my niece, the only one in the family who could speak English, informed me.

Here, I fitted in; I knew who I was. In England, I felt peeved at being four foot ten. I had always wanted to be five foot two, as that was just about a respectable height! In Germany, with my family, however, I fitted in perfectly – my grandmother was only four foot six, my aunt four foot eight, so at four foot ten, I was tall. Since that visit, I have been content to be just 'a little extra'.